Valley Forge

Books by Donald Barr Chidsey

NOVELS

His Majesty's Highwayman
This Bright Sword
Captain Bashful
Lord of the Isles
Captain Adam
Stronghold
Panama Passage
Nobody Heard the Shot
Each One Was Alone
Weeping Is for Women
Pistols in the Morning

BIOGRAPHY

Elizabeth I
John the Great: *The Times and Life of John L. Sullivan*
The Gentleman from New York: *A Biography of Roscoe Conkling*
Sir Humphrey Gilbert
Sir Walter Raleigh
Marlborough: *The Portrait of a Conqueror*
Bonnie Prince Charlie: *A Life of the Young Pretender*

JUVENILE

Rod Rides High

Valley Forge

By

DONALD BARR CHIDSEY

CROWN PUBLISHERS, INC.
NEW YORK

Fourth Printing, May, 1966

Library of Congress Catalog Card Number: 59-9156

Printed in the United States of America

Contents

Valley Forge

Chapter One

CAMP FOLLOWERS, by command of the general, were forbidden to take part in the parade. They must go around Philadelphia, fittingly with the baggage. Only the soldiers themselves, and their officers, also the pioneers carrying spade and axe, and the musicians busily using their instruments, George Washington had decreed, should march that radiant August 24, 1777. There were eleven thousand of these, and they were strung out in such a way as to make them look more. Each wore a bit of greenery in his hat. This again was by direct order from the Commander in Chief, who was hopeful that this, the first full public appearance of his charge, might serve to shore up a wobbling cause.

Of the thirteen colonies, now become by declaration independent states, twelve had troops in that line of march; and even the thirteenth—faraway, sparsely populated Georgia—was represented by individual patriots, such as, for example, peppery Lachlan McIntosh, a brigadier general who a little while ago had killed Button Gwinnett, the Signer, in a duel.

Their immediate goal was Darby, where they were to camp; but within a few days they would range themselves between the immensely superior force of Sir William Howe, even now landing at the upper end of Chesapeake Bay, and Howe's objective, Philadelphia. It was not a pleasant prospect. Yet the spirit of the men was high. Down Front Street they went, and over Chestnut. They laughed and sang, waving.

> "O, how joyful I shall be
> When I get the money!
> I will bring it all to thee,
> O, my diddling honey!"

They were scrutinized.

"They don't step exactly in time," one spectator, John Adams, was to write his wife that night. "They don't hold up their heads quite erect, nor turn out their toes so exactly as they ought."[1] Adams was captious, as always. In fact the display, meant to impress the strong Tory element in Philadelphia, was a success.

Those who had arms carried them every which way, and indeed the weapons themselves were of many kinds and sizes. Most of the officers wore swords, and some—some of the sergeants as well—carried spontoons, or spears, suitable for stopping a man who had a bayonet; but of bayonets themselves—though bayonet work was the particular pride of the British army—there were few.

A great many of the men carried shovels or picks or both, for this was the *diggingest* rabble that ever had been known, a fact that was subject of many a jape in the British ranks, where except under actual siege conditions a trench or redoubt was considered somewhat sissified. There were also in evidence, that day on Broad Street, a large number of axes, polished for the occasion and carried jauntily, like muskets, across the shoulder. These were not medieval, not meant to be weapons. They were for felling trees to make road blocks, for razing or building bridges, most of all for the erection of breastworks. Your Continental always liked to get *behind* something when he fought.

A little group of frontiersmen here, another there, carried the long, deadly Kentucky rifle, a weapon invented (by some unknown genius) and manufactured in Pennsylvania, not Kentucky. These were superior in accuracy and in reloading time to the clumsy rifles the Hessian jägers carried; but there were pitifully few of them.

There had been a movement in Congress, a movement backed by the hardheaded Benjamin Franklin, to equip the army with longbows. There were many reasons for this. The colonies lacked metal, but they did have plenty of wood. Bows would be much cheaper, much quicker to produce and to replace. It took a man years to learn to be a gunsmith, but bowyers and fletchers could be trained in a matter of weeks, and their equipment was lighter and more easily moved, so that they could stay with an army in motion. Weather was always unpredictable, and a shower could take the firing power out of a whole army as neatly as a housewife snicks the spine from a mackerel; but rain would not balk an archer. The longbow, as developed in the mountains of Wales in the twelfth century and never improved upon, even when accompanied by a large quiver of arrows weighed less and was more convenient to carry than the gun, ramrod, mallet, wadding, cartouche box, powder horn, pincers, mold, lead, and scales of the musketeer. It made no sound and gave forth no smoke to betray the archer's position. There was no chance of a misfire, a flash in the pan; no chance either of a flareback at the touchhole in the event of a shifting wind, something that had cost many a musketeer his eyebrows or even his eyes. Arrows were recoverable, bullets were not. Unlike the bullet, the arrow could be seen coming—this was a point made much of by Franklin—and so might serve to frighten the enemy. An arrow discharged by any able archer would pierce an inch of solid oak at more than two hundred yards. A musket ball, if it could be made to carry that far—something less than one hundred yards was its ordinary killing range, and it was wildly inaccurate even then—would be spent, incapable of causing a man even to stumble. Best of all, the trained longbowman could discharge twelve, fourteen, sixteen arrows in the time it took the man with the musket to reload.

The movement was lost. The musket prevailed. It was not a standardized military gun, like the British brown Bess, but a weapon of varying length and varying weight, anywhere from thirteen gauge to thirty gauge, made, no doubt, at some local blacksmith's shop and bearing very little resemblance to its neighbors to right and left. The parts were not interchangeable. Neither were the bullets, which had to be cut separately for each separate gun, as the powder had to be separately measured and wrapped—a waste of time in the best of circumstances, under battle conditions impossible. It was this lack of uniformity of weapons, more than any other one thing, that caused foreign military observers to shake their heads, calling this the most inefficient army that had ever been put into the field.

Good soldiers the Americans certainly were, the European professionals averred, or at least could be if they were properly led, equipped, and trained. *Natural* soldiers, yes—but business men? No! As further evidence of the lack of preparation and the appalling mismanagement,[2] a large number of the soldiers, perhaps almost one-fifth, carried no weapons at all.

They didn't seem to mind. Marching four abreast, with a step that was light and gay if not remarkable for crispness, they waved to the women in the windows.

"We are the troop
That ne'er will stoop
To wretched sla-ver-y."

At least they were clean, shaved, their hair freshly clubbed. Not many, except among the officers, wore even a hint of military insignia. Their coats were of many colors, but some had none, marching in their shirtsleeves. When General Washington went by, tall, grave, unbelievably handsome, it was observed all down the line that he wore the uniform he had made famous as a member of the Continental Congress just before he'd been appointed commander in chief. This was the uniform selected by the Virginia militia regiment of foot of which he was colonel. The coat was blue turned over with buff, which were also the colors of the military group of Alexandria, Virginia, of which the Commander in Chief was colonel ex officio. Such other officers who favored blue, however, generally preferred a darker shade and different facings. For instance, the uniform of the Delaware Continentals, John Haslet's regiment—and many of the men were wearing it—was a dark blue turned over with dark red, a uniform almost identical with that of the Hessians; this similarity had resulted, at Harlem Heights, in a body of redcoats falling in with them—to find themselves prisoners.

The predominating color that afternoon in Philadelphia, however, was brown, butternut being favored. The nearest thing to a uniform was the hunting shirt, which actually *was* the authorized uniform of certain frontier groups. Many a man who had never done any hunting wore this, an eminently sensible garment, usually long-skirted and made of linen. George Washington himself—pointing to the convenience and accessibility of the hunting shirt, as well as to the fact that from a distance it might strike fear into the hearts of the British, who could think all who wore it frontier marksmen —favored the hunting shirt when no other uniform was authorized or available. He did this in an official order. He also recommended what he called overalls: long, loose trousers of the same color and material as the hunting shirt, gaiterlike at the base and fastened by straps under the instep. There was God's plenty of overalls in Philadelphia this day.[3]

The musicians for the most part were in the middle, strung out like the men themselves to make them look greater in number. They were not very fancy, though they did play with vigor. None of them carried a trumpet or a set of bagpipes, nor was there even so much as a bugle to be seen; and if any of these men had encountered any of the instruments issued to the Guards and many other British regiments—clarinets, oboes, bassoons, horns—he wouldn't have known what to make of them. No, the Continental army musicians had only the fife and the drum. But they did well with these.[4]

> "Over the hills with heart we go
> To fight the proud insulting foe.
> Our country calls and we'll obey—
> Over the hills and far away."

And so the army marched . . . and marched . . . to the banks of the Brandywine.

Chapter Two

THEY MET the enemy and were whipped. But there was no disgrace. Outnumbered, outmaneuvered, nevertheless they retreated well, snapping. They were inexpert, true, but they weren't cowardly. Men on both sides had predicted that when you got the Yankee out from behind his barricade, up out of his ditch or trench, and faced him with a disciplined force, he'd run. On the banks of the Brandywine this was proved to be not true. There was plenty of fight left in the Continentals.

Two weeks later, September 27, Sir William Howe occupied Philadelphia.

This amiable roué, a cousin of the King on the left hand, was always excruciatingly slow. He had taken New York. Philadelphia was an even brighter prize. Here was surely a greater town in size, in trade, in every way—the wonder indeed of the West, a center of learning, a hub of commerce, America's pride. In population alone, being surpassed only by London, Philadelphia was the second largest city in the English-speaking world. Moreover, until the other day when Congress had ignominiously scampered for the cover of York, Pennsylvania, eighty miles west, Philadelphia had been the capital of this shaky but cocky new country.

Capturing an enemy's capital often marks the end of a war.

Among his many other advantages, Howe had a navy. For the capture of New York the British had sent to sea by far the biggest fleet in history—man for man, ship for ship, and in tonnage and in cost, much larger than the Spanish Armada. Many of the vessels, mere chartered transports, had returned or had gone elsewhere; but the warships remained, immeasurably more powerful than anything the colonists could launch. Moreover, this force was commanded by General Howe's own elder brother, Richard, Lord Howe (Black Dick). With a languor that must have been a family characteristic,[5] Admiral Howe had carried his brother and most of his brother's men from New York down the coast to Chesapeake

Bay and up that bay to its northernmost navigable point, Head of Elk (now Elkton); so that the redcoats, after brushing aside Washington's army, had approached Philadelphia from the south. Once there, Howe paused, pleased.

"The British have taken Philadelphia," Franklin, in Paris, was told.

"No, sir; Philadelphia has taken the British."

For he knew the town well, none better. It was a friendly place, and by no means priggish, despite the Quaker element. The streets were most marvelously clean and straight, the shops opulent. The newcomers were not hailed as liberators, yet neither were they spat upon. They could be comfortable in Philadelphia, save for one thing—there was no food. Howe had brought supplies with him, but he couldn't stand an indefinite siege, and the townspeople themselves were begging for provisions. The sea door of Philadelphia had been closed by some ingenious but not very stout blocks and also by two strongholds, Fort Mifflin and Fort Mercer. Until Howe could again make contact with his brother, insuring a regular maritime supply service, he was in trouble. This was rich countryside, but the Continentals, instead of accepting their defeat, swarmed everywhere like angry bees. Foraging parties had to be in great force, and even then they were likely to find little.

Army and navy alike, therefore, went to work on forts Mercer and Mifflin.

Except among his own men, who adored him, George Washington was in low favor. It was said of him (Princeton and Trenton being forgotten) that he had had nothing but defeats, and that though he might have been a good Indian fighter in his time he was not up to the realities of modern field warfare. The cause, with New York and Philadelphia in British hands, wobbled. An eminent clergyman, a former Congressional chaplain, wrote to the Commander in Chief to point out the hopelessness of the Continental position and to urge him to avert bloodshed by suing for peace. There were a good many others who felt that way. The British were simply too strong, the Continental army too weak.

So Washington attacked.

It was a stroke brilliantly planned, a three-pronged surprise at dawn of the main British army encamped at Germantown. With better trained men and more experienced officers, and also with luck in the weather, it might have succeeded in smashing Howe then and there, which almost certainly would have ended the war. As it was, Continental columns lost touch with one another; parties fired on one another; bypassed pockets of British resistance were heard to be shooting still and were mistaken for an enveloping movement in force. Worst of all, fog crept in from the river.

The surprise was complete, the first attack a splendid success, but then came the fog and confusion, giving the British a chance to steady, their officers a chance to steel them. Training began to tell. The redcoats refused to stampede; they ceased to retreat; they stood and at last, on command, they advanced.

The Continentals were driven back. They lost a lot of men, a lot of guns, and even more prestige.[6]

They were still full of fight. Though their rearguard had been mauled at Paoli (only a few miles south of Valley Forge), where the British superiority with the bayonet was made sickeningly clear, though supplies were short in their miserable camp at Whitemarsh, when Howe marched out of Philadelphia they all but ran to meet him. Weather called off this encounter. It rained for two full days and nights, so that not a man on either side had any powder he could use.

Howe came forth yet again, and again the Continentals, dug in and ready, waited confidently. But the British general, after a good look, decided that they were secure, and he went back to Philadelphia, a much more comfortable place.

It was the end of the season. The campaign was over.

The British were all right. Mifflin and Mercer had fallen, November 16 and 20, and supplies again were coming in by sea. Howe, lazy but by no means incompetent, had thrown a formidable hoop of defense works around the city. The British could settle down and enjoy themselves.

The Hessians under his command were wont to grumble

that if Howe were being paid by the job instead of by the day, the war wouldn't last so long; and when it was rumored that he might be raised to the peerage for having taken Philadelphia, the title of Lord Delay-ware was suggested.

With the Continentals it was otherwise. Not only was there no city to shelter them, but they maintained no base; nor was there money with which to pay them, or food, or clothing. Besides, they had obligations. They could not afford to sit back and wait. They must harry all Brittish foraging parties. They must watch Philadelphia like a cat a mousehole, at the same time protecting all that part of Pennsylvania, Delaware too, and Maryland, and New Jersey. The small, crabapple-sharp Abraham Clark, a member of Congress from Elizabethtown, wrote to General Stirling: "We have been much alarmed by a report that the Army was going into Winter quarters in or about Wilmington, thereby leaving New Jersey and a great part of Penns[a] intirely open to the Enemy."[7] Stirling undoubtedly showed this letter to George Washington, as he must have been meant to do.[8]

Most important of all, they had to stay in existence. The soldiers had courage, but they also had stomachs: they were human. This army might dissolve at a sneeze, and once it fell apart it could never be put together again. There was no question of fighting. They would not even have a chance to fight unless they somehow survived until spring.

Chapter Three

"DE L'AUDACE, *encore de l'audace, et toujours de l'audace,*" was a cry George Washington could not have heard, nor would he have understood it if he had; for he knew no French, distrusted the French. But to the sentiment he would have subscribed.

He was at this time studying still another plan—a plan for attacking the British in Philadelphia itself and wresting the capital from them.

Here was rashness incarnate, and it is hard to see how it could have resulted in anything but tragedy. Likely enough the Commander in Chief had little faith in it, but he was a conscientious man, aware of his own shortcomings and always eager to ask, as he was often willing to take, the advice of others. He put this plan before his general officers in council assembled, November 24. He asked them to submit their opinions in writing.[9]

Eleven were opposed, and only four—Stirling, Scott, Wayne, Woodford, a major general and three brigadiers—were in favor. The plan was dropped.

There were alternatives. At least one officer, Casimir Pulaski, the Pole, favored somehow keeping the army in motion.

Greene, Lafayette, Armstrong, Smallwood, Wayne, and Scott wanted a camp at or near Wilmington, Delaware; in the end Smallwood was stationed there with a mobile brigade, an effective nuisance force. But it was no place for the whole army, being flat, vulnerable, and easily cut off from the supplies of the north.

There was a line from the Schuylkill to Bethlehem, which had a few supporters, and a line from Reading to Lancaster, which had more. Originally Stirling, Knox, Sullivan, and "Scotch Willie" Maxwell were the only ones in favor of Valley Forge, a third suggestion.

"We have not yet determined upon a position for the Army during the Winter," Washington wrote to Horatio Gates from the headquarters at Whitemarsh, December 2; later that day he wrote the same thing to Joseph Reed.

The truth is, a great deal of pressure was being brought upon Washington. Congressman Clark was not alone. There were many who were suspicious of a standing army, a federal force, and dubious about the wisdom of having any commander in chief at all—or at least of having one man for more than a few months at a time. Authority just then was a touchy subject. Hadn't Oliver Cromwell too been a mild-mannered, unambitious, quiet country gentleman before he tasted power? Yet—each one wished to have his own cows protected.

On November 28 Congress appointed a committee to confer with General Washington on the winter campaign, and December 16 this committee reported back, its report being that exactly nothing had been done.

The following day the Pennsylvania legislature addressed a remonstrance to Washington insisting, in effect, that all of the state's property be guarded. Wearily the General replied: "It would give me infinite pleasure to afford protection to every individual and to every Spot of Ground in the whole of the United States. Nothing is more to my wish. But this is not possible with our present force."

And to Congress he wrote: "I can assure those Gentlemen that it is a much easier and less distressing thing to draw remontrances in a comfortable room by a good fire than to occupy a cold bleak hill and sleep under frost and Snow without Cloaths or Blankets."

The committee's report was not correct. The army by that time had started for Valley Forge, thirteen miles from Whitemarsh. Had it waited too long? It was in pitiful condition, the men barely able to stagger, many without shoes, all of them hungry and cold, for the quartermaster's department as well as the commissary appeared to have broken down. What's more, it had no ordinary supplies, not even tents, these having been sent a little earlier—at a time of fear of a British attack—to Trappe, eighteen miles to the northwest.

The first day, laboriously, they covered three miles, bivouacking on the ground at a place called the Gulph.

Albigence Waldo, a surgeon, a Connecticut Yankee, had not been enjoying himself. "Provisions & Whiskey very scarce. Were Soldiers to have plenty of Food & Rum, I believe they would storm Tophet," he wrote in his diary December 8. Four days later the tale was even grimmer: "Sun Set—We were order'd to march over the River—It snows—I'm sick—eat nothing—No Whiskey—No Forage—Lord—Lord—Lord." But when he reached the Gulph the surgeon was really discouraged. ". . . not an improper name neither, for this Gulph seems well adapted by its situation to keep us from the pleasures and enjoyments of this World, or being conversant with any body in it. It is an excellent place to raise the Ideas of a Philosopher beyond the glutted thoughts and Reflexions of an Epicurean."

"We had no tents, nor axes to cut wood to make fires," reported Ebenezer Wild in *his* diary. "It was a very bad snow storm when we stopped."

Next day the snow changed to rain, and the wind rose, so that it was bitterly cold. The tents did arrive, but by that time everybody was soaked to the skin, and still there was no firewood.

At night the rain froze, making the road impassable for an army so poorly shod.

The day after that they would not have been permitted to march even if they'd been able to, for it was set aside by motion of Congress to give thanks to God for the victory in the north, Saratoga. There were prayers, and there was some show of parade. There might even have been a few songs; but the men's teeth were chattering, for there were no fires, and the rain never paused.

They stayed four days in that hole—four days of unmitigated misery—and when at last, on the nineteenth they made the few remaining miles to Valley Forge, they assumed that the worst was over.

This was a mistake.

Chapter Four

DEFENSE WAS the first consideration, not comfort. An outsider might have wondered why anybody should even make an effort to stamp out this rabble of uncertain, lousy, sick, bleeding men. Yet they were the very heart of the Continental cause, and its only hope. Were they struck a smart blow now, they'd be smashed. Their problem, as they arrived at that grim hill, was not to gird themselves for the fray, but simply somehow to stay alive.

The place was twenty-odd miles from Philadelphia—near enough to threaten any foraging party, far enough to provide against the possibility of a forced night march, a surprise attack at dawn.

It was very strong—a long high plateau. It might have been designed by a military engineer.

The Schuylkill bound the north and part of the east and west. A shallow sleepy stream, nowhere wide, in many places fordable, and likely to be solid ice in the middle of winter, it nevertheless made a stout palisade for almost half of the camp site—and that for two reasons. Because it was on the north, the British, if they were to sally forth from Philadelphia, would be obliged to make a wide half-circling movement in order to attack across the Schuylkill; also, the ground sloped sharply up from the south bank, and the summit could be fortified.

To the east and south, the direction of Philadelphia, lay flat land with no cover, land scowled at from the heights along the river. Still, this was the direction from which an attack might most likely be made, as it was the most convenient, the widest, the nearest; so artificial barriers were called for.

That was the way they came, up the old Gulph Road, with the muck almost indistinguishable from the fields on either side, through the village King of Prussia, and up the long, long slope, every step of which must have been an agony.

The western border of the camp was the Valley Creek, a pretty creek of no military importance. The Valley Creek ran northward through a deep and very narrow gorge in which it would have been impossible to mount artillery, maneuver with cavalry, or even deploy any considerable body of infantry. The west, moreover, was the farthest from Philadelphia, about twenty-two miles.

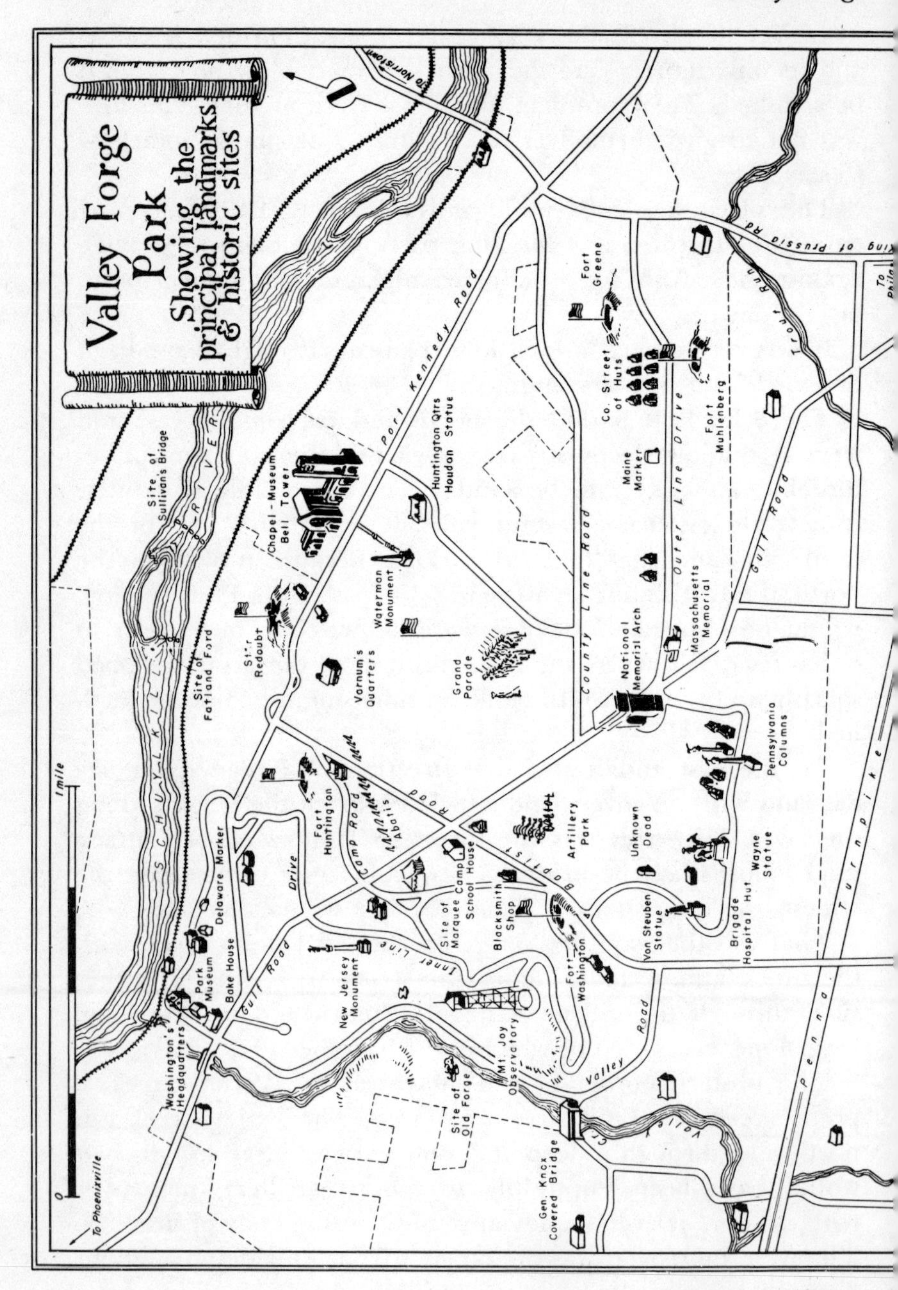

Courtesy Valley Forge State Park Commission

Where the Valley Creek tumbled into the Schuylkill was the village that was to give the camp its name.

This village—a handful of houses, no stores, and the forge itself a short distance up the creek—had not been permitted to snooze in pastoral peace. The forge—not merely a blacksmithy but, as the word was used then, a complete iron-making unit: bloomery, finery, chafery, slitting mill—operated by two Quaker families, the Dewees and the Pottses, until recently had been an important source of supply for the Continental army, which in addition had maintained a magazine there. For this reason the small place, after the battle of the Brandywine, had caught the attention of the British, who visited it in force and spent three days there, the men camping on the very hill now selected for the Continentals. The weather had been mild then, late September. The British, taking their time, had burned everything that they could burn and stolen everything that they could steal.[10] Though some of the buildings, being of stone, had resisted ravishment—Mrs. Deborah Hewes's house, for example, which was to be the General's headquarters—Valley Forge when the Continentals came upon it was a ghost town.

"I have from the Beginning view'd this Situation with Horror!" General Varnum was to write to General Greene after a few months of it. "It is unparalelled in the History of Mankind to establish Winter Quarters in a Country wasted, and without a single Magazine."[11]

It was rich farm country, the Valley Forge advocates might have retorted. And truly it was. But the British had paid that call. . . . The forge would never work again,[12] and the surrounding countryside had been currycombed.

The hill was thick with trees—black oaks, giant white oaks, hickory, and cedar suitable for shingles (then called "shakes"); but there wasn't much else. The ground could be used to make mud for cementing chimneys built of logs; but it was uncommonly hard and cold to sleep on.

This country is lovely in the summer, in the spring, or the blazing season of fall. It must have been unspeakably bleak when the Continental soldiers first saw it, December 19, 1777.

On either side of the Valley Creek there is a peak exceptionally high for that part of the country. They are not twins, though they are similar. The smaller one to the west is called Mount Misery, the other Mount Joy.[13] It was to bring about many a jest that the one located *inside* the camp was Mount Joy. But one may doubt that this raised laughter the first day; there was too much to be done.

Chapter Five

HUTTING—the word was in everyday use—at least was a way of keeping warm. Some preparation had been made. General orders of December 18 specified that all non-commissioned men be broken into squads of twelve. Each hut should harbor that many. It should be fourteen by sixteen feet, the walls six feet six inches high. The sides and ends should be made of logs, the roof of planks. Nothing was said about the floor, and in practice few of the huts had any. The fireplaces were to be made of fieldstone, chinked, like the logs, with mud. Chimneys were optional.

"I was there when the army first began to build huts," Tom Paine wrote to Ben Franklin in Paris. "They appeared to me like a family of beavers; everyone busy; some carrying logs, others mud, and the rest fastening them together."[14]

The Commander in Chief offered a reward of one hundred dollars out of his own purse to anybody who would invent or discover something better than boards—which took time to make—for the roofs. Nobody ever did.

The first squad to finish its hut in each regiment was to get twelve dollars. Axmen were at work right away, and the very first hut was reared by the end of the second day in camp. However, others took much longer.

Washington was a great believer in prizes, bonuses, in cash as an incentive. He was untiring in his efforts to get more pay for the soldiers, or at least to get them what was due them. "Men may speculate as they will," he wrote to Congress in this connection. "They may talk of patriotism. . . . but whoever builds upon it, as a sufficient Basis for conducting a long and bloody War, will find themselves deceived in the end. We must take the passions of Men as Nature has given them, and those principles as a guide to which they are generally the ruler of Action. I do not mean to exclude altogether the Idea of Patriotism. I know it exists and I know it has done much in the present Contest. But I will venture to assert, that a great and lasting War can never be supported on this principle alone. It must be aided by a prospect of Interest or some reward. For a time, it may, of itself, push Men to Action; to bear much, to encounter difficulties; but it will not endure unassisted by Interest."[15]

General orders for December 29 earnestly exhorted officers "of every rank to use their utmost exertions to have the huts completed as soon as possible, that the troops may get comfortably lodged."

Washington himself refused to take a house at first but caused his marquee to be pitched on the camp site; he lived there for almost a week, after which he moved into Deborah Hewes's house at the northwest corner of the encampment, near the junction of the Valley Creek and the Schuylkill.

He worried about the men. ". . . many . . . are not yet under Cover," he noted sadly on January 3.

The following day there was a general order stating, "As fast as the men go into Hutts the tents are to be returned immediately to the Quarter Master General."

February 8, in a letter to Brigadier Thomas Nelson, Jr., Washington wrote: "We have lost a good many men, and Horses, by hard fare in our present Quarters; but hope we have seen the worst, especially with respect to the first, as most of the men are now in tolerable good Hutts."

A tolerable good Hutt was no palace. Seldom was there any

floor but the packed earth. Often the wind could get through, and did; for this was a high exposed site. Few of the fireplaces drew well, and even with those there was a great deal of choking smoke in the hut, for the wood was green. Many of the soldiers spent a great deal of their time—even their sleeping time—out of doors, crouching around a fire, eyes reddened, fingers stiff, turning now this way, now that, in an effort to keep from freezing. The huts faced one another in streets, grouped by brigades, and often the men of two huts, or even three or four, would band together to keep up a great fire all night. This waste of wood was made necessary by the lack of blankets. Anyway, there was plenty of wood, neither the quartermaster's department nor the commissary having anything to do with this. The men themselves chopped down and trimmed the trees. Hauling in the logs was harder. The horses, unstabled, starved, were dying in droves, and those that survived were weaker than the men. There were no wagons. Building sledges was difficult and time-consuming, even when materials could be had. For the most part the men were their own beasts of burden, blessing what snow there was when they dragged the logs in from the hills, cursing of course when there was none. Anyway it kept a soldier busy, kept him from going numb.

Valley Forge—Original Company Street showing Muhlenberg Huts.
Courtesy Valley Forge State Park Commission

The dead horses—it was a backbreaking task to bury them with the ground frozen—presented a problem in sanitation. So did the latrines.

Valley Forge was not haphazard. It was a military city, the huts in neat rows. Provision had been made for latrines, which were early dug and banked, each some distance from any hut. But it was hard to get the men, especially at night, to go so far from the fires. Some, thinking of that knife-like wind, would relieve themselves in the camp street. Others wouldn't even go out.

Many of the huts, as a result, stank. Brigadier Anthony Wayne, a well-connected tanner of those parts, used to say that he hated his inspection trips and would rather have gone into battle each week; but he was a fighting fool anyway, a salamander.

The purpose of the January 4 order, commanding return of the tents to the quartermaster general as soon as a hut was completed, was clear enough. Tents would rot unless cleaned and kept in a dry place. They must be made ready for the time when the army would march again, leaving its huts behind.

But it was a hard order to enforce; and that not only because the men hated the quartermaster's department—why shouldn't they?—but also, and even more, because they cut up the canvas and used it for socks, for undershirts, anything in an effort to keep warm. Repeated orders went out to bolster the first, but as late as the middle of May headquarters was still trying to get those tents back.

Not only were the men cold, they were hungry. ". . . not Long since our Brigade drue But an half Days aLownce of Meat in Eight Day But these Defeltis the men Bore with a Degree of fortitude Becoming soldiers," Captain Hodgkins wrote to his wife back in Ipswich, Massachusetts.[16]

There were no onions, even for headquarters, until the second week in January, and not many then. There were a few potatoes and cabbages, and even a few turnips—at one and a half dollars a dozen—but no coffee, tea only at twenty dollars a pound *gold,* no milk, no whiskey (one gill of rum was issued to each private and N.C.O. on New Year's Day, but there had been none at all on Christmas), and in the middle of a rich farming country no eggs. Butter cost a dollar a pound, when there was any.

Major General Nathanael Greene, a short pleasant man from Rhode Island, a learned blacksmith, remarked that the people of the United States evidently expected their soldiers to eat air.

Desertions understandably increased. It got to the point where Washington glumly warned Congress that if those conditions continued "we shall be obliged to detach one-half of the army to bring back the other." Yet it is worth remarking, as it was remarked at the time, that most of those deserters were not native Americans but men who had previously quit the British army or else men who had lately come to America—"old-country men," as the phrase of the day had it. The loyalist lawyer Joseph Galloway in March reported that 1,134 deserters from the Continental army had entered Philadelphia since the beginning of the occupation, September 27; but three-quarters of them were foreigners.

The army urgently needed three to four thousand blankets and could use more, Washington warned the Board of War early in January. The board appointed another committee but it didn't get any blankets.

He had almost three thousand men unfit for duty by reason of a lack of shoes or clothes, also "many others detained in Hospitals and Crowded in Farmers Houses for the same Causes."

When the British made a foraging raid in force toward Darby, December 22, Washington, though he knew about it in time, was unable to raise enough able-bodied men to intercept them.

A pint of milk, a quart of beer, peas, beans, butter, a pound of bread, and a pound of either meat or stockfish, were supposed to be alloted to each man each day. What they actually lived on for a long while was fire-cake. Fire-cake was flour mixed with water and, when it was available, a little salt, and heated on a griddle. It was not very tasty.

"Ye who Eat Pumpin Pie and Roast Turkies, and yet Curse fortune for using you ill, Curse her no more," wrote Surgeon Waldo in his diary, December 22, "least she reduce your allowance of her favours to a bit of Fire Cake, & a draught of Cold Water, & in Cold Weather too."

That same day George Washington in a plea to Congress referred to the "alarming deficiency or rather total failure of Supplies," and the following day, on a note all but hysterical for him, he wrote: "Unless some great and capital change suddenly takes place in that line, this army must inevitably be reduced to one or other of these three things—Starve—dissolve—or disperse."

Chapter Six

GREAT BRITAIN had not declared war, for that would have been to recognize the colonies as an independent state. The colonies, for their part, insisted that they were not engaged in war but only defending themselves against brutal and illegal aggression. Thus there was no formal beginning of this fight. The day of Lexington-Concord is the most convenient, as it is the most realistic.

That had been two and a half years before the Continental army made its camp at Valley Forge. All war is sinfully wasteful, appallingly expensive, and inefficient. The colonies, as represented by the Continental Congress, went into the conflict unprepared, true; and, in the belief that the fighting wouldn't last long, they shifted from one expedient to another, causing great confusion. But at the end of two and a half years it might be thought that any system would have straightened itself out, at least enough to avert disaster. There will always be crooked army contractors, and eighteenth-century folks were not at all squeamish about such things, for it was an age of corruption; yet in the Continental army of the Revolution—in sober fact an army made up of patriots—there seems to have been amazingly little official theft. Why, then, after two and a half years, were the men reduced to such straits?

The answer is not simple.

The army had grown out of nothing. It had no background, no traditions. Washington himself had been but a colonel of militia with a short record of Indian fighting. Only a handful of his fellow officers—Gates, Charles Lee, a few foreigners—had ever been in a regular army. Nor had Congress, an extralegal body in the first place—the British soldiers called it King Kong—ever handled anything even remotely like a war.

In the beginning the office of quartermaster general was set up for transportation, while that of commissary general was set up for the purchase of provisions. As in the British army, our natural model, the men were expected to buy their own uniforms, but in practice, again as in the British army, the government did this for them. When replacements were needed and the men were far from home, how else could it be arranged? Congress on June 17, 1777, had created the office of clothier general.

The first commissary general was Joseph Trumbull of Connecticut, and he was a good one, very good. Oldest of the four talented sons of Jonathan Trumbull, governor of Connecticut, he knew his countinghouse as he knew his goods. He drove himself. Indeed, he could be said to have driven himself into the grave; for after two years of it his health gave way, and he resigned, to die.[17]

He must have been an extraordinary man. Alone among those in the war movement he never was called a liar, a cheat, or even a fool. Not many knew him—he was a quiet, preoccupied person, muttering his figures—but everybody had a good word for him, and after his resignation all sorts of measures were taken in an effort to get him back.

". . . we were supplied from hand to mouth and frequently not at all, from the day Mr. Trumbull left the Commissary department," Washington wrote to Governor Livingston of New Jersey, February 14.

And General Greene wrote to his brother Jacob, January 3, that "the army has been fed from hand to mouth ever since Mr. Trumbull left it."[18]

"I have heard it asserted by more than one sensible, disinterested man, that the removal of Mr. Trumbull from that office has been the source of all our misfortunes," young John Laurens, one of Washington's secretaries, wrote to his father, the president of the Continental Congress.[19]

Trumbull was succeeded by William Buchanan, who does not seem to have co-operated closely with headquarters. Washington, in a letter to Congress urging appointment of a committee to reorganize the army administration, refers to Buchanan as a man "whom I rarely see."

In another department the Congress was lucky. A German gingerbread specialist who lived and had his shop in Philadelphia, staunch Christopher Ludwig, was offered the post of superintendent of bakers and director of baking, the proposal being made that he produce 100 pounds of bread for every 135 pounds of flour furnished him. Mildly but firmly Ludwig replied that he had made all the money he needed, and if he took the job he would supply 100 pounds of bread for every 100 pounds of flour. He did, too, throughout the war, though there were times at Valley Forge when no flour arrived; once in February there were six such days on end.

It was not good policy to depend upon exceptional persons, as Congress recognized when, on May 14, 1777, it adopted a twenty-section report on reorganization of the quartermaster general's department.

Congress admittedly had deteriorated.[20] It was not the distinguished body of men it once had been. Many of its best members—George Washington, John Sullivan, Christopher Gadsden, Patrick Henry—either had taken to the field or had returned to their state capitals, judging this work the more important. Yet it still contained many an experienced lawyer; and how such a group ever came to adopt this masterpiece of impenetrability, an instrument almost guaranteed not to work, it is difficult at this distance to see.

Section 5 provides: "That no forage master, to whose care any magazine of forage shall be committed, shall issue any part thereof unless by a written order of the commander in chief, the commander in chief of the department, the commanding officer of the post where such a magazine may be established, the quartermaster general or deputy quartermaster general of the department, or one of his assistants, the waggon master general or any other waggon master; such orders to specify to whose use the forage is intended; and every such order to be filed by the forage master, and a regular entry to be made thereof in a book to be by him kept for that purpose, as a voucher for the expenditure of the forage by him received."

Section 10 decrees: "That the waggon master general of the army, or waggon master in any of the departments thereof, shall receive from the quartermaster general or deputy quartermaster general of any department, all such horses, cattle, and carriages as the service shall require; and that neither the waggon master general nor any other waggon master shall, on any account, presume to purchase any horses, cattle, or carriages for the public service, without the express order of the commander in chief, the commander in chief of the department, the quartermaster general or deputy quartermaster general of a department; nor shall the waggon master general, or any other waggon master, hire any horses, cattle, or carriages, unless by the authority aforesaid, or by that of an assistant deputy quartermaster general."

The last section sets the rates of pay for the quartermaster general (though at this time Washington was complaining that he seldom saw that personage either) and for his assistants. The quartermaster general was to get 166 dollars a month,[21] in addition to his pay as a major general.

Soon afterward Congress reorganized also the commissary

general's department. It did this in a bill of forty-one sections, few of them intelligible, running to about six thousand words and crammed with references to duplicate invoices, receipts, issuance slips, ten-columned ledgers, etc., etc.

Section 16 provided: "That every Creature purchased for the Use of the Army shall immediately thereafter be branded with the initial Letters of the purchasing Commissary's Name and the first Creature purchased by said Commissary shall be branded on the horns with the Figure 1, the second with the Figure 2, and so on."

Not until later did the men in the field begin to point out that hogs don't have horns, and neither do hens. This difficulty was righted in an amendment, October 4.

The trouble was not so much in getting food and clothing as in getting them to the places where they were needed. Previous to the war, what communication there was between these non-manufacturing colonies had been carried on largely by way of the sea, the coastal waters; but now a British fleet commanded this avenue. The roads were abominable, in winter largely impassable. Contractors were demanding forty-five shillings a day for wagon, driver, and four horses; but Congress was only willing to pay thirty.

Transportation was in the province of the quartermaster general, that brilliant, erratic, contentious, cantankerous, opinionated young orator, Thomas Mifflin.

The ragged ones at Valley Forge could hardly have known much about Mifflin, whose talents were political rather than military; but if they felt the need of a villain, here he would have been—in part because their plight would seem the fault of the chief of supply, in part because the man showed opposed to the one person the ragged ones all trusted: the Commander in Chief.

Chapter Seven

IN THE MIDDLE of it all sat George Washington, that sphinx, around whom controversy raged. There were no charges, not even whispered ones. It was a matter of personality. It was almost a matter of religious faith.

The Commander in Chief himself, a man of intense reserve, must have been embarrassed by the passions he roused.

In part this feeling was sectional. The New England members of Congress, and particularly John Adams, a man "unhappily incapable of seeing conspicuous merit in anyone but himself,"[22] and his cousin Sam, had never ceased to regret that hard political necessity had caused them to vote for a Virginian. At worst they had hoped that this would prove a temporary measure. Now it was congealing into permanency, and they were alarmed. They didn't like Washington's coolness, his insistence upon respect to rank, any more than Washington liked their "leveling," which he considered not merely bad manners but downright dangerous.

Washington was a snob, but he did not let his snobbery affect his judgment at headquarters. He might or might not have had his private opinion of some of his staff officers, which might or might not have flattered them, but so long as they did their work he treated them well, even intimately, no matter where they came from or what had previously been their station in life. Henry Knox had been a bookseller, Nathanael Greene a blacksmith, while John Glover of Marblehead, Massachusetts, (it was his outfit, crack boatmen, that had rescued the army from the trap at Long Island, and later had taken care of both of Washington's celebrated nocturnal crossings and recrossings of the Delaware) before the war had been a fisherman. Washington treated them as he treated those successful New England lawyers, John Sullivan and James Mitchell Varnum. From his own state were two brigadiers, Peter Muhlenberg, a Lutheran preacher, and George (Calabash Joe) Weedon, who formerly had kept a small country inn; neither of these had any cause to complain of discrimination at headquarters.

Indeed it is notable that all denigration came from outside. Those close to Washington never dreamed of distrusting him.

There is little doubt that this adoration—it could hardly be called less—was at least in part responsible for the suspicion with which George Washington was regarded by certain members of Congress.

Those closest to him, not the general staff officers but his aides and secretaries, were young men, most of them under thirty, and exceedingly, even fanatically loyal: in their eyes anybody who didn't worship Washington was a traitor. Not without reason, they thought well of themselves. They were dedicated and voluble. These lieutenant colonels—John Laurens, Alexander Hamilton, John Fitzgerald, Tench Tilghman, Caleb Gibbs, Robert Hanson Harrison, Richard Kidder Meade, John Walker—handled Washington's correspondence and arranged his appointments. They were not well liked.

The first of these bright young men, and the only one who didn't stick it out,[23] was Thomas Mifflin.

He had money, position, looks, wit. He came from a mercantile family, and had been abroad. He was persuasive. He could think on his feet. At the age of twenty-eight he was elected as one of Philadelphia's two representatives in the Pennsylvania legislature, the other one being Benjamin Franklin. It was no more than natural that when Washington was appointed commander in chief and prepared to go to Boston and take charge of the siege, he named Thomas Mifflin his aide-de-camp. Everybody—including, assuredly, Mifflin—predicted a glorious future for the young man.

He rose rapidly and soon was a colonel, then a brigadier, and the first quartermaster general of the Continental army.

He did not want the job, and hadn't asked for it. He was greedy for glory, which he assumed could be won only on the field. But Washington, needing him, would not give him a command.

Mifflin thought the quartermaster-generalship tedious, per-

Thomas Mifflin (in later years). *Courtesy New York Public Library Picture Collection*

haps even debasing, and he resigned it as soon as he could; another clever young man, Stephen Moylan, "an accomplished Irish gentleman resident among us, but of habits and manners not exactly suited to the difficulties of the time,"[24] took it over. For one reason or another Moylan did not last, and Mifflin was induced to take the quartermaster-generalship back, though he did the work with his left hand.

Then a curious thing happened. Washington sent Mifflin to Philadelphia to confer with Congress and to give it a clear idea of conditions on the field. Mifflin had so many friends there, and in short order made so many more, that Congress decided to keep him on hand, and sent a formal note to Washington—it amounted to a command—requesting Mifflin's services as an adviser.

Congress raised Mifflin to a major-generalship, but still he didn't get that independent command.

There was never to be an open quarrel between Washington and his original aide, but the split was clear, as was the reason for it.

Though he had recently bought a home in Reading, Pennsylvania, Mifflin was first of all a Philadelphian, and when Howe had quit Boston and it was not certain whether he meant to attack New York next, or Philadelphia or Charleston,

Mifflin hurried north from Congress to advise the Commander in Chief to let the others go but at all costs to defend Philadelphia, the pride of the New World. As was his wont, Washington listened to all advice. Another major general, Nathanael Greene, significantly a New Englander, was prominent among those who urged the defense of New York and the Hudson River. Mifflin took it personally, as though Greene had insulted a lady he loved, and he never did forgive Greene, whom he accused, as did others, of unduly influencing the Commander in Chief. Washington himself kept his mouth shut.

Mifflin was vehement about it. We have no record of what was said at those staff meetings, but it seems certain that young Mifflin waved his arms, raised his voice. At any rate, afterward he appeared to think that he no longer had any chance of getting a division, which would depend upon Washington, so he returned to Philadelphia and to his politicking.

Undeniably he was good at that, a tower of strength to the patriot cause, raising money, enlisting men, serving on all sorts of committees, keeping the Whigs in line, the Tories at bay. But as for the quartermaster-generalship, he hardly paid any attention to it but administered it through deputies at long distance.

Early in October, 1777, after threatening for some time to do so, he resigned the office, giving ill health as his reason, and retired to Reading. Congress, however, did not accept the resignation. Congress didn't do anything about it at all, for there was another plan in the wind, as Mifflin himself knew. He was not doomed to sulk long in Reading.

The appointment of a Board of War, November 7, was a move meant to help, not to hinder, George Washington. Congress for some time had realized that it was overextending itself, that the war should be run by professionals; and Washington had approved the idea of having a Board of War instead of the previous Congressional committee. The board, a full-time group, should contain no Congressmen.

Mifflin was appointed among the first, apparently with Washington's concurrence, as were also Colonel Timothy

Pickering of Massachusetts and Lieutenant Colonel Robert H. Harrison of Maryland.

Harrison, thirty-two years old, was Washington's military secretary, having more or less taken Mifflin's place, and his appointment was undoubtedly meant to reassure the Commander in Chief. The secretary of the previous committee Richard Peters of Pennsylvania, was held over. Mifflin presumably was slated to be the chairman.

Harrison, however, asked to be excused. He didn't think he knew enough, he said. More likely he was reluctant to leave the commander.

On November 27, Horatio Gates was appointed, and was named president of the board.

It looked, at least to Washington's friends, like a slap in the face of the Commander in Chief.[25] Gates was the victor at Saratoga, the hero of the hour. Aside from Charles Lee, who happened to be a prisoner of the British, he was the only American who had held any mentionable position in the British army. He was easy-going, even sloppy, popular with the soldiers, yet at the same time an admirable disciplinarian, something men said Washington could never be.

If any one was being considered as a successor to George Washington it was Horatio Gates.

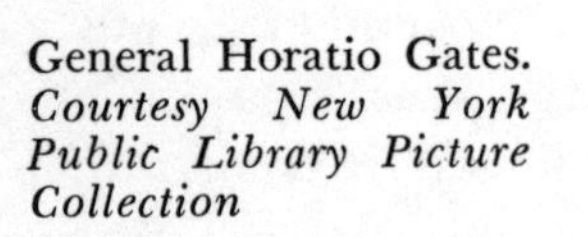

General Horatio Gates. *Courtesy New York Public Library Picture Collection*

When, for some reason not now clear, Peters withdrew and James Wilkinson was appointed secretary, then the Washington faction waxed shrill. Wilkinson, just turned twenty-one, had been raised to a brigadiership at the insistence of Horatio Gates. He was one of Gates's own bright young men.

The day after the board was appointed, Congress at last got around to accepting Mifflin's resignation as quartermaster general, though it permitted him to keep his rank of major general without its pay (but he was to get two thousand dollars a year as a member of the Board of War). This solved nothing; for the very next day the board put Mifflin in charge of the quartermaster's department, leaving everything where it had been before.

It was hard on the men in the huts.

Chapter Eight

David Bushnell of Saybrook, Connecticut, was a man with a bee in his bonnet. He believed that it was possible to make an enclosed boat that could be operated under water. In 1776 he had actually built such a monstrosity and called it the *Turtle*.

It was made of oak planks banded with iron, and was seven feet long, four feet wide, eight feet high—just large enough to hold one man. Whether on the surface or submerged, it moved in an upright position. The bottom was weighted with seven hundred pounds of lead, and there was also a water tank down there and two small brass forcing pumps, worked by foot, for bringing in or pushing out liquid ballast. At the top was a tiny conning tower, its sides consisting of slabs of glass. This was just large enough for a man's head. There was no periscope. The stem and stern were like the lips of a clam. Forward, outside, operated by means of a hand crank and a pedal arrangement, was a small screw propeller, the first in history.

The Turtle. *Courtesy New York Public Library Picture Collection*

This propeller was of the "puller" type. Astern, moved by an inside tiller, was a rudder. The craft could go backward or forward, depending upon which way the crank was turned. There was a smaller screw propeller mounted on top of the conning tower. This, geared to a separate crank, was for diving or rising.

Bushnell, a Yale man, was nothing if not ingenious. Previous machines designed to slam an "infernal" or "water petard" against the side of an enemy vessel had been hit-and-run contraptions. Bushnell proposed to approach the vessel in silence, coming up beneath the hull. The infernal itself, a waterproof sack of gunpowder rigged with floats to make it buoyant and operated by a clock mechanism—possibly the first time *this* was ever used—could be detached from the inside of the *Turtle,* whether submerged or on the surface. The biggest problem was how to prepare a niche for it underneath the vessel to be destroyed, so that it wouldn't slip away or be carried off by the tide. For this purpose Bushnell had made a strong borer, a pointed screw, also operated from the inside, with which it was planned to drill a hole in the ship's bottom. The infernal would then be released, to nestle into this aperture, and the *Turtle* might go away.

Stealth was necessary. The *Turtle* could have been sunk by almost any sort of fire, conceivably even by musket fire.

At the last moment the man trained to operate it, Bushnell's own brother, Ezra, fell ill. Another Ezra, Ezra Lee, a sergeant in the Continental army who came from Lyme, Connecticut, was substituted.

Early in the morning of a September day in 1776, Sergeant Lee set forth on his extraordinary journey. His goal was the flagship of Admiral Howe's fleet, the sixty-gun *Eagle,* at anchor near Governor's Island in upper New York Bay. He could show no light, but the needle and card of his compass were smeared with phosphorus.

The tide was stronger than he had expected. Nevertheless he reached his target unchallenged. He dived, and came up underneath the warship. He started to work his bore. It wouldn't work.

Many British vessels of war at that time, having just come from or being destined to go to the West Indies or some other tropical place, had copper-sheathed bottoms to guard against the teredo worm. The *Eagle* was one of these; but this possibility had been anticipated, and the borer was designed to be strong enough to bite right through the sheathing. But what-

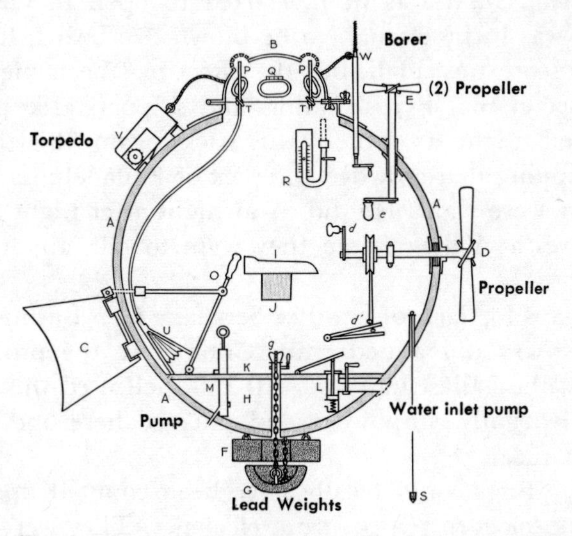

Plan of the Turtle. *Courtesy New York Public Library Picture Collection*

ever it was Sergeant Lee had come up against—one of the iron strips bracing the rudder post?—he couldn not make a hole in it.

He tried to shift to another spot, but the bore, blunted, was stuck. He was running short of air. Because of the tide he was far behind schedule, and it would soon be daylight. Also, the infernal was about to go off.

He retreated.

Hailed from a patroling smallboat, he released the infernal which blew up with a terrific bang, waking everybody in the fleet and giving Lee a chance to make good his escape.

Thus the first try was frustrated, though it did throw a scare into the British, among whom all sorts of wild rumors darted.

Bushnell, who at least had proved that gunpowder could be exploded under water, put his *Turtle* aside after another abortive attempt, and built a different infernal, which with a whaleboat he strove to drive against the side of the frigate *Cerberus* off New London, Connecticut, August 15, 1777. It fell short, and was seen and hauled up on deck. Four sailors, wondering what was in it, started to open it. One of these sailors was lucky enough to be blown overboard; he survived.

The score was small, but the effect had been big. It was an open secret that British sailors and skippers alike feared that Bushnell might try some of his tricks again, this time against the shipping that crowded the port of Philadelphia.

They were right. He did. And night after night around the campfires at Valley Forge they were to talk about it—and to sing.

Perhaps for lack of another Sergeant Lee, Bushnell now decided to try unmanned craft. Gone were the propellers and rudder, the ballast tank too. All Bushnell used this time was a keg filled with gunpowder and plugged here and there with contact fuses.

These fuses could hardly have been counted upon for fifty per cent, or even ten per cent, efficiency. They were ingenious, but unreliable. Each consisted of a peg driven half through a hole in the keg; at a sharp jar this peg would set off an ordinary cocked musket firing-lock inside, and the ensuing spark would cause the whole business to blow up—maybe.

It could even be that Bushnell did not expect the things to go off, except occasionally and by accident, and was counting upon the moral effect, a follow-up of the scare the *Turtle* had caused. Perhaps that was why he used forty kegs, floating downstream.

The theory was that whatever damage they did would hurt the British, since all shipping was either British war vessels or else vessels in the employ of the British.[26] Even if only one went off, it might bring about a panic.

Only one did, and it did.

The kegs were launched upstream during the first days of January, 1778. It was a poor time. The ice had broken, and the Delaware at Philadelphia was filled with large chunks of it. For this reason the warships, which ordinarily would have been anchored in midstream, had been pulled out of harm's way to one shore or the other. Some boys saw one of the first kegs, and went after it in a rowboat. One or perhaps both were killed; the reports were vague. But an alarm had been raised. The cry of "Infernals!" went up, to be echoed everywhere. Soldiers stationed along the waterfront, whether or not they had been ordered to do so, began to discharge their muskets at every bit of flotsam they could see among the floes. Part of this shooting might have been because they were bored, as soldiers on guard duty so often are; but the story told in the Continental camp was that the shooting went on wildly for a day and a night, and that the redcoats had used more powder blasting away at the kegs—and not hitting any—than the kegs themselves contained.

This tale tickled a small jumping jack of a man named Francis Hopkinson, painter, poet, patriot, politician, musician, lawyer, member of Congress from New Jersey, and designer of the Stars and Stripes, who rendered the episode into gleesome verse; and when on March 4 the *Pennsylvania Packet* published "The Battle of the Kegs," a great Continental victory had been won.

It was wrong and it was ragged, but it was undeniably funny, and it felt good to the soldier who sat on a bleak hill-side.

> "Gallants attend, and hear a friend
> Trill forth harmonious ditty.
> Strange things I'll tell, which late befell
> In Philadelphia city."

Hopkinson was an accomplished composer but, perhaps from lack of time, he did not make up the music for "The Battle of the Kegs," pitching it instead to "Yankee Doodle," an air everybody knew.[27]

> "Some fire cried, which some denied.
> But some said the earth had quakèd
> And girls and boys, with hideous noise,
> Ran through the streets half naked."

The thing swept the country, but nowhere was it more popular than at Valley Forge, where the Continentals bawled it to a star-studded sky, scarcely able to wait for their favorite verse:

> "Sir William, he, snug as a flea,
> Lay all this while a-snoring;
> Nor dream'd of harm as he lay warm
> In bed with --- ------
>
> "Now in a fright, he starts upright,
> Awak'd by such a clatter;
> He rubs his eyes, and boldly cries
> 'For God's sake, what's the matter?' "

The lady needed no introduction to soldiers of either camp. Though Hopkinson in the original printed version—it was re-printed many times as broadside and handbill—had followed the custom of pamphleteers and left carefully measured blanks, when it came time to sing that verse nobody hesitated to cry "Mrs. Loring."

Born a Lloyd, she had been described as a "dazzling blonde." Howe met her in Boston, and the conquest could hardly have taken long. Loring, himself a loyalist, was immediately mollified by appointment as commissary general of prisoners, a sinecure that enabled him to misappropriate about two-thirds of the rations, getting rich at the expense of his confined fellow-countrymen, hundreds of whom he starved to death. Loring traveled with headquarters; but everybody knew where his wife slept.

After the evacuation of Boston she had followed Howe to Halifax, later to New York. Now she was with him in Philadelphia, where she had been dubbed "the Sultana." She loved strong drink and high stakes, as did her protector. Inevitably it was said that the success of the American arms owed a great deal to the success of hers.[28]

> "The fish below swam to and fro,
> Attack'd from every quarter.
> 'Why sure,' thought they, 'the devil's to pay
> 'Mongst folks above the water.' "

The boys loved it, and so did their betters, and it was even said that when Francis Hopkinson sang it one night to General George Washington, the General, who so seldom even smiled, guffawed. That was a good sign.[29]

Chapter Nine

THERE WAS one man in camp who, far from wasting away, amazingly expanded, though he had been large in the first place. From the beginning of that winter Henry Knox, chief of artillery, was both figuratively and literally in the middle of things at Valley Forge. A bookseller from Boston, he had a deep voice, a florid complexion, and almost unbelievable energy. He was romantic too, madly in love with his plump wife, Lucy, the daughter of a prominent loyalist, with whom he had eloped. Two hundred and fifty quick-moving pounds when at the age of twenty-five he had joined the fight as a colonel, he was to pick up thirty-odd more before the war ended, though how many of these might have been put on at Valley Forge is not a matter of record.[30]

Among the mutterers in Congress, the men who knew their Roman history and trembled in fear of the emergence of a military dictator, the name of Henry Knox often was linked with that of Nathanael Greene as one who must be swaying the Commander in Chief the wrong way; for just as in England it was customary to excuse the weaknesses of King George by blaming his ministers, so at York when anybody dared to decry the Washington record it was done obliquely, circuitously: certain staff members were responsible, not the General himself, who was only misled.

Knox and Greene did have much in common, though Greene was the senior both in age and military rank. Each was self-educated, with no previous war experience, an ingenious improviser, a whirlwind of activity, incalculably ambitious. Each was trusted by Washington. Each was a New Englander who couldn't abide a fool—and did not mind saying so. In consequence, they had many enemies. Of all the so-called "sinister influences" at headquarters, these two were declared the worst. They probably didn't care, being too busy.

Of Greene it is also remarkable that, like his bitterest enemy,

Thomas Mifflin, he had been voted out of the Society of Friends because of his military labors.

Another energetic large man who was close to the Commander in Chief, and so suspect, was John Sullivan of New Hampshire. Red of face and short of temper, he couldn't sit still. There were those who contended that Major General Sullivan was also short of brains, and undoubtedly he was a man of action rather than a man of thought; but Washington believed in him, and so did the soldiers. When a slam-bang fight was called for, Sullivan was your man. He liked nothing better than to slug it out, toe to toe. Valley Forge, with its enforced idleness, was an agony to him.

". . . we have got our hutts allmost Don for the men But its Reported that Genl How intends to Come & See our new houses & give us a House warming But if he should I hope we shall have all things Ready to Receive him & treet him in Every Respect according to his Desarts," Captain Hodgkins told his wife in a letter.[31]

But—with the huts and earthworks finished, what was left for the men to do?

Henry Knox had established an artillery park and a blacksmith's shop in the camp, but there was precious little equipment to maintain. Drills were haphazard, held at the whim of brigadiers and colonels, who, however, seldom attended them. The hauling-in of fuel, to be sure, was an unremitting labor. There was routine sentry duty. There was also lookout duty. Since horses were few and supply and scouting parties could not be relied upon, a series of tall trees—most of them oaks but there were a few chestnuts—was utilized, platforms or half-barrels, rather like the crow's nest of a ship, being erected high in each, where men were stationed night and day. Foraging of course was ceaseless. And just hugging a fire and trying to stay alive was an occupation in itself.

Nevertheless the situation was serious. There was no provision for entertainment or sport of any kind. There were no regular churches. Fishing was negligible, the hunting nonexistent. Though a country gentleman who did not mind risking a careful coin now and then when in the company of friends, the Commander in Chief took dice and cards to be bad for military morale, and they were strictly forbidden. There were no dances, there being nobody to dance with. There were no bars, not even many bottles. Officers were reminded of the saying that the Devil finds tasks for idle hands to do.

John Sullivan, a major general, met this emergency by having his men build a bridge over the Schuylkill.

The order for this went out of headquarters December 23, but the actual work did not start until the middle of January.

A great part of the foraging and all the evacuation of the sick took place to the north and west of camp, beyond the river, and there was little likelihood of attack from that quarter; such a bridge would be easy to defend anyway. The river was fordable at many points, one of the best being at Fatland, fairly in the middle of the northern line of the camp; but ice in winter and perhaps freshets in the spring—if spring ever came—might make this awkward and sometimes even dangerous, especially for carters. All the same, it is probable that one of the chief reasons for building the bridge—which was called Sullivan's Bridge—was to keep the men busy, to keep them working and thus warm.

Log piers were driven into the bottom, and these were protected against ice and high water by means of stone-filled boxes. The floor of the bridge itself was made of split logs, flat side down. The bridge was twelve feet wide. It could hardly have been handsome, but it served its purpose and the men were inordinately proud of it. Each pier was dedicated to one of the major generals in camp. In the middle, very deep, was carved the year—1778—for the men who made it were sure that it would last for a long while.[32]

Chapter Ten

"THE LAST campaign furnished sufficient proof that the stubborn and inexperienced rebels are too lucky," the adjutant general of the Hessian forces on January 20 wrote to his patron, whom he addressed as "Right Honorable Lord, Gracious and Mighty Major General."[33]

A little earlier, on Christmas Day, a German on the other side, Johann Kalb, had written to *his* patron, De Broglie: "How sad, that troops of such excellence and so much zeal, should be so little spared and so badly led!"[34]

"We want nothing but good officers to constitute as good an army as ever marched into the field. Our men are much better than the officers," Nathanael Greene stoutly told his boss.[35]

Lucky or badly led or what not, the Continentals—every foreign observer remarked it—were a *slovenly* pack. Nothing about them glittered. They slouched, their salutes languid, while the casual relations between officers and enlisted men were never less than shocking.

In the circumstances, the camp at Valley Forge was a most amazingly peaceful one.

There were many reasons for this.

It was situated in farm country, and no city or even sizable village was near, while the farmers themselves and the members of their families, though doubtless in many respects admirable, were hardly *jolly* neighbors. Of "ammunition wives" there were few. On January 6 an order went out from headquarters that no private horses would be tolerated in camp, and two days after that there was an order that there should be no dice or card playing, "under any pretence whatever." These orders were pretty well kept.

Nor was there much drunkenness. For a time this might have been accounted for, at least in part, by the fact that the sutlers charged so much and the men had so little money; but on January 23 general orders provided for brigade sutlers with a set scale of luxury prices: peach brandy 7 shillings 6 pence a quart, 4 shillings a pint, 1/1 a gill; whiskey and applejack, 6/ a quart, 3/6 a pint, 1/ a gill; "cyder," 1/3 a quart; strong beer, 2/6 a quart; common beer, 1/ a quart; leaf tobacco, 4/ a pound; pigtail tobacco, 1 dollar a pound; hard soap, 2/ a pound. On the whole, these prices appear to have been enforced.[36]

There are almost no reports of out-of-bounds brutality and rape. There were complaints—few farmers enjoy seeing their livestock driven away for a handful of worthless paper money—but not against the personal behavior of the men.

Even petty theft does not seem to have been common, possibly because there was so little to steal. Organized thievery was dealt with harshly—and promptly. When Denham Ford, a commissary in Greene's division, was convicted of theft, he was drummed out of camp, literally. For an unspecified offense, though probably a similar one, Lieutenant Elson of Colonel Malcolm's regiment was drummed out of camp with his coat reversed, a scene Lt. James McMichael found "shocking."[37]

On February 5, a Lieutenant Grey, convicted of stealing, was ordered to be publicly thrown out of the army, his sword first being broken over his head.

Though the men at Valley Forge came from all parts of the new nation, there was little of the sectional hatred in the ranks that had marked the first Continental encampment before Boston and that was to prove the curse of the army of the north. Most of these men were not militia but professional soldiers, and proud of it. They saved their ferocity for the foe.

Dueling was forbidden, though of course practiced—but not often.

"This day with most of the officers of Gen. Greene's division I accompanied the corpse of Lieut. Green to Upper Merion, where it was interred with the honors of war," records Lieutenant McMichael of the Pennsylvania line. "He was a gentleman of an amiable disposition, who unfortunately was mortally wounded in a duel with Lieut. White." That was April 30. Earlier, Lieutenant Sugars had been cashiered just for having challenged Lieutenant Jacob Laudermilk; but

Washington, doubtless with the shortage of officers in mind, restored him to his rank.

Perhaps because there were so few militiamen at Valley Forge, the crime of bounty-jumping—enlisting, collecting the enlistment bounty, deserting, enlisting under another name and collecting *that* bounty, etc.—was not common, as it was in New England and northern New York, where recently one soldier had been convicted of repeating this process *seven times.* He was shot.

The articles of war Congress had adopted listed fourteen capital offenses, but in fact there were few persons executed that winter at Valley Forge.

The worst crime, as it was the commonest, was desertion. This was somewhat narrowly defined, and included men who had only strayed out of camp and failed to return in time. However, there were varying degrees of punishment, and for *desertion to the enemy* the noose was prescribed. Unexpectedly, this also applied to civilians, who were strictly forbidden to cart their produce into Philadelphia where they would be paid in gold. Several civilians were hanged for this, and many were flogged. Washington's reluctance to offend the civilian population did not extend to this form of "desertion." Again and again he refused to issue a pardon in such a case, or to moderate the punishment. And it could be that here his harshness paid off. In Philadelphia the military got most of their supplies by sea, and though these could scarcely have been exciting they were substantial; but the townspeople had to beg —or pay through the nose. Beef had gone from five to twenty-five pence a pound; a chicken cost ten shillings; the price of flour had trebled; brown sugar, the only kind there was, sold at six shillings a pound, chocolate at five shillings.[38]

There is no record of any man at Valley Forge being forced to run the gantlet, one of the more disgusting of the military punishments in vogue. There is only one case of an order for salt water to be thrown over the bleeding back of a man who had just been flogged; and this too was, if not customary, at least not unusual elsewhere.

Flogging was an accepted practice. It was horrid, and certainly it was ineffectual; but nobody could think of anything better.

Moses' law was the rule at first. Like many another unadmirable custom, Moses' law had Biblical authority. "Forty stripes he may give him, and not exceed" (Deut. 25:3). "Of the Jews five times received I forty stripes save one" (II Cor. 2:24). The second rather than the first of these quotations formed the basis of Moses' law, which was, as for so many years on land and sea it had been, thirty-nine well laid on. The average pirate or slave of this and the preceding centuries was not familiar with the derivation of the phrase—but he knew what it meant.

It became worse. Congress, in June of 1776, increased this limit of thirty-nine to one hundred, and incorporated the change into the revised articles of war adopted September 20 of that year—an increase made if not at Washington's insistence at least with his consent, for he was known to believe that thirty-nine was "inadequate." Washington was sometimes blamed for babying his men, and the charge rankled.

The restriction appears not to have been lived up to, for there were four culprits sentenced to two hundred and fifty lashes each at Valley Forge on January 22, and one to two hundred lashes.

Even this was moderate. British punishment, designed for the jailbirds, who made up a good part of the imperial armies then, were more prolonged. A marine in Boston, November 24, 1775, got eight hundred lashes for striking a lieutenant. On January 3, 1776, a private got a thousand, while his "wife" got a hundred plus three months in the guard house, the charge being theft. Two of Burgoyne's men got a thousand each at Fort Edward, "in different portions of the most conspicuous parts of the town." The publicity of these affairs was stressed, it being an essential part of the idea of punishment then; the whole company or even regiment, together with as much of the civilian population as it was possible to corral, watched. Because there would be no sense in whipping a man who was unconscious—and regulations called for a surgeon always to be on hand—such a heavy sentence might extend over several days, even a week. Once in the British navy a man who had been flogged around the fleet died with fifty lashes still to come—and his captain ordered the sentence to be completed upon the corpse.[39]

Today we shudder. They didn't then.

There was work to be done at Valley Forge, and though general orders of January 15 had authorized the construction of a jail, there is reason to believe that it was not much used.

Reveille was at dawn. It was beaten on a drum, as all such signals were, there being no bugle. Troop was at eight, retreat at sunset. Tattoo (from the Dutch *Tap toe,* from *Doe den tap toe,* or "Put the tap to," meaning in early seventeenth-century slang "Stop!" "Cease!" "Shut up!") depended upon the time of year; but always it was soon after sunset. It meant lights out. There was no taps, a later development.

With it all, the men didn't complain much. They could take it.

Chapter Eleven

THE DAWN was opalescent, September 4, 1778, when four men climbed a fence into a meadow outside of Harrison, New York. Two, carrying black bags, bowed to one another. The others remained aloof.

When the seconds had decided that it was light enough, and had paced the field and loaded the guns, the principals, facing one another for the first time, threw off their cloaks.

They were both rather short. Until a little while ago they had been intimate friends; but now they stood on the field of honor.

Horatio Gates was fifty, James Wilkinson twenty-one.

"One, two, three—*fire!*"

The pistols came down, or started to. Wilkinson, whether purposely or from excitement, fired into the air. Gates leveled, but when he pulled the trigger there was only a flash, no explosion.

The silent seconds—Thaddeus Kosciusko, the Polish patriot, for Gates, John Barker Church for Wilkinson—reloaded.

"Fire!"

Wilkinson fired, and missed. Gates didn't stir.

Wilkinson's pistol was made up again. The seconds stepped back.

"Fire!"

Wilkinson missed. Gates, a crack shot, took his time aiming. He pulled. There was that firing-pan flash again—nothing more.

Then, since the business was getting on everyone's nerves, the men shook hands and called it off.

In a larger sense, of course, the last shot in the affair known to history as the Conway Cabal, never will be fired. Historians will always squabble about it.

It should no more have been named after Thomas Conway than the western hemisphere should have been named after Amerigo Vespucci.[40] He, Conway, born in Ireland, had been brought up in France and was a soldier by profession. It is probable; though he never had a chance to prove it here, that he was a good soldier. It is certain that he was a poor diplomat.

That anomaly, a gullible Connecticut Yankee, Silas Deane, together with Arthur Lee ("One of the most suspicious, the most atribilious, and the most cantankerous persons whom the Revolution produced . . . with an extraordinary power of hating, an endless fund of acrimony, and an exhaustless capacity for lying, he did an amount of evil out of all proportion to his very moderate ability."[41]), were responsible for Conway's crossing of the sea. These two were our agents in Paris, and when they were instructed to ship over some army engineers and organizers, they, especially Deane, responded with an exuberance that all but swamped the states with pompous, penniless, arrogant, bemedaled adventurers.

Conway at least could speak English.

He was forty-four, and he felt so sorry for the poor stupid struggling Continentals that he consented to accept a commission as a mere brigadier general, though he pulled every political string to raise this to a major generalship—a rank, he said, more nearly commensurate with his European status.

He had no sense of humor. His fellow brigadiers in the camp—this was before the move to Valley Forge—shocked him. He would look at one, then another, and another, asking each time in genuine amazement: "Did Congress see you before they appointed you?" He was not beloved. James Mitchell Varnum of Rhode Island, who had a handsome library and who could carry on a conversation in Latin as readily as in English,[42] though sometimes in the presence of strutting Europeans he put on "homespun" airs, once snappishly told the newcomer that for all he knew there might be generals in America as capable of carrying on a campaign as was King Frederick of Prussia. Beyond all doubt Conway then assumed that he had fallen among madmen, for didn't everybody know that Frederick the Great was God?

Washington took an immediate dislike to the man, and was crushingly proper in his presence. Conway, miffed, appealed to Congress, which passed his complaint back to the Commander in Chief.

"If General Conway means, by cool receptions . . . that I did not receive him in the language of a warm and cordial friend, I readily confess the charge," Washington replied. "I did not, nor shall I ever, till I am capable of the arts of dissimulation. These I despise, and my feelings will not permit me to make professions of friendship to a man I deem my enemy, and whose system of conduct forbids it. At the same time, truth authorizes me to say, that he was received and treated with proper respect to his official character, and that he has had no cause to justify the assertion, that he could not expect any support for fulfilling the duties of his appointment."[43]

There was more here than peevishness. Conway was a disturbing influence on the staff. A previous French adventurer,

Du Coudrai, by his high-and-mighty airs had caused a threat of resignation on the part of two of Washington's most valued generals. The whole *staff* might quit if Conway got out of hand.

Officers were in short supply. Washington was deadly serious when, February 14, turning down Sullivan's request for a furlough, he pointed out that he had only two other major generals in camp, where there were then fewer than ten thousand men, and in consequence was confined to headquarters by "an uninterrupted series of Business." According to the new military establishment that was shaping up at this time, the Continental army soon would have, in a given infantry regiment, a colonel, a lieutenant colonel, a major, six captains, a paymaster, an adjutant, a quartermaster, a surgeon, a surgeon's mate, eight lieutenants, nine ensigns, a sergeant major, a quartermaster sergeant, twenty-seven sergeants, a captain-lieutenant (over the colonel's company), a drum major, a fife major, eight drums and fifes, twenty-seven corporals, 477 privates—a total of 585.[44] And Washington was earnestly urging that the number of lieutenants should be doubled.

Officers were leaving in droves. It was hard to see how they could be kept, for in many ways they suffered worse than the men. They had not been in peacetime a special breed, a privileged class. Many had been elected to their posts as the militia officers were elected—by popular vote. Their commissions were not disposable for cash, salable, like British army commissions. Their pay was not greatly in excess of that of the men, and their expenses were skyrocketing. They might survive somehow at camp, though miserably, by going into debt; but man after man among them—and this applied from lieutenants right up to the major generals—was getting letters in which his wife cried out that she didn't see how she and the children could survive another week. Prices at home, too, had gone 'way up. Local communities in general made it a practice to support or at least give out some sort of dole to deserving families of privates and non-coms; but no such arrangement ever was made for the families of officers.

There might have been another matter in the back of Washington's mind about Thomas Conway, and probably there was. He could write to Richard Henry Lee that "His [Conway's] importance in this army exists more in his own imagination than in reality," but in fact he must have been worried.

Of the two British army veterans in the Continental cause, both of them presently major generals, one, Charles Lee, an eccentric, coarse-mouthed, dog-loving man, clever as the Devil, had the previous summer fallen into the hands of the British and was now a prisoner in New York, though Washington was bending every effort to have him exchanged and this might soon happen. The other was Horatio Gates, upon whom the public was lavishing hysterical praise.[45]

There was plenty of talk that one or the other of these men might make a better commander in chief than Washington, who had tried and failed. It wasn't loud talk, but Washington knew about it. His own friends no doubt were making it worse by their adulation.

Thomas Conway could hardly be thought of as a third possible candidate, but if he were allied with either of the others such an alliance could be formidable. Conway might lack tact, but he did have prestige. His military record was impressive. He was reputed to be strongest, too, as was Gates, in the very matters in which Washington admittedly was weak—discipline, organization.

Conway would not be a candidate, no. But he might serve as a cat's-paw.

Washington watched him.

After the battle of the Brandywine it was generally reported that Conway had written a letter—to whom?—setting forth fourteen different military errors the Commander in Chief had been guilty of that day. Other reports said sixteen, or twenty-three. Anyway, the letter was much talked about, though nobody ever would own to having seen it.

Some Congressmen were openly sarcastic. Sergeant, lately of New Jersey, wrote to Lovell of Massachusetts, Nov. 20, 1777, that Washington had been guilty of "such blunders as might have disgraced a soldier of three months standing." James

Lovell himself, a waspish man opposed to practically everything, wrote to Gates: "I have reason to think the battle of Germantown [as discrediting to Washington] was the day of salvation offered by Heaven to us." Later Lovell wrote to Sam Adams, who was also anti-Washington, relative to a resolution passed by Congress December 10, "You could not expect more smartness in a resolve which was meant to rap a Demi-G over the knuckles."[46] John Adams was even more outspoken. On the very floor of Congress he said: "I have been distressed to see some members of this house disposed to idolize an image which their own hands have molten. I speak here of the superstitious veneration that is sometimes paid to General Washington."

The Commander in Chief waited. Outwardly imperturbable, in fact as edgy as a racehorse, he could not make any move—it wouldn't be dignified—until he caught them in a misstep. So he watched, waiting.

And then young Wilkinson got tight—and talked.

Chapter Twelve

THIS WILKINSON was another prodigy thrown up by the war, and a malodorous one. Of fox-hunting Maryland stock, he had been trained as a physician in Philadelphia and had practiced for a little while; but his heart was in the army, and at the news of Bunker Hill he marched off. Preferring or professing to prefer field work, he found that he had a natural aptitude for the tasks at headquarters. He was in demand as an aide-de-camp—to Greene, Arnold, then Gates. Sent north as a captain, he rose rapidly, rank by rank, until at the age of twenty he was a lieutenant colonel and Gates's adjutant.

In this capacity he conducted the dickering with the cornered Burgoyne, and it was he who actually introduced Gentleman

Johnny to General Gates at the sword-handing ceremony, though it was Burgoyne, that glittering macaroni, that playwright, who stole the show by bowing, by lifting his hat, with: "The fortune of war, General, has made me your prisoner."

General James Wilkinson (in later years). *Courtesy New York Public Library Picture Collection*

After that it was no more than natural that the General's protégé, carrying with him the General's request that he be jumped two grades to a brigadiership, should take to Congress the official news of the victory, an assignment that customarily carried with it, besides promotion, some sort of gift—a scroll, a sword, what not.

He took his time, enjoying himself, for he was made much of. "Wilkinson's Canter" this was called. The distance from Albany to York, Pennsylvania, where Congress was then sitting —whether or not he meant it as a personal snub, Gates did not take the trouble to report officially to his Commander in Chief until some time later—is about 285 miles, the way Wilkinson went. Though he was well mounted, he took sixteen days to do it—a performance that caused one Congressman, when the question of a gift came up, to suggest a pair of spurs.

It was in Reading, Pennsylvania, that he made the slip.

He had stopped over, but next day it was raining, and when General Stirling suggested another night, offering dinner, Wilkinson snapped at the chance.

William Alexander, though a major general in the Continental army, claimed the title Earl of Stirling. The British parliament did not allow this claim, but everybody in the colonies did, and he was known as Lord Stirling, while his wife was miladied. Bald, bluff, affable, he set a famous table. But he had a fault. In the felicitous phrase of the day, he was "not responsible after dinner." His was "the most martial appearance of any General in the Service. . . . He is mild in his private Conversation, and vociferous in the field."[47] Wilkinson himself was to write that "his addictions were notorious and his fondness for a long set not the least remarkable, for no man could be more strongly disposed to fight his battles over again."[48]

Just now Stirling was bored, inactive as a result of a fall from his horse, and he welcomed the chance to entertain young Wilkinson, as did his aides, McWilliams and Monroe. These four sat late, and at last Wilkinson told Monroe and McWilliams—his lordship had presumably passed out by this time—about a certain letter General Conway had sent to General Gates, a letter in which Conway expressed an exceedingly low opinion of the Commander in Chief.

Monroe was discreet, as became a future President, and he made no mention of this next day, even after Wilkinson had resumed his amble. Not so McWilliams, who blabbed. Now, Lord Stirling was a man whose mind never was befogged by indecision. He saw his duty. He wrote to Washington.

And Washington wrote to Conway:

"Sir: A Letter, which I received last night, contained the following paragraph: 'In a letter from Genl. Conway to Genl. Gates, he says: "Heaven has been determind to save your Country; or a weak General and bad Counsellors would have ruined it." ' I am, Sir, Yr. Hble Servt., G. Washington."

The curtness of this would suggest a challenge, or at least an expression of willingness to accept a challenge, but no such course was conceivable in the circumstances. Not only was Washington known to be opposed to dueling, perhaps even in peacetime, but it was the custom in all services of all nations at that time that only those who were equal in rank could meet on the field of honor, and that for obvious reasons no officer, no matter what the provocation, might challenge his superior.

No, Washington would not fight. He left that to the others, whose fighting, however, was largely verbal—and frenzied. The attitude of those involved was like that of little boys about to be spanked. They seemed to cry, each of them: "I didn't do nothing but I won't do it again!" Gates, in a long explanation that explained nothing, first denied that he had received such a letter, then seemed to admit it, though he didn't produce the letter itself. Nobody ever did see that. Gates and Conway had never met, as both pointed out, but Conway admitted that he had opened a correspondence with Gates. At first Conway denied having written anything like the weak-general-and-bad-counsellors letter; then he said that he might have; and finally he said, what of it? He was careful to point out, and more than once, that abroad it was the custom for junior staff officers to draw up papers criticizing their seniors on purely technical military grounds, which papers would be passed about and discussed. This did nothing to convince Washington's friends, who didn't believe it anyway, nor did it decrease the unpopularity of Conway, who was seen to be back in his old habit of starting every third sentence with "Now, in Europe—"

Conway, December 13, over Washington's fervent objections, had been raised to major general and made inspector general of the army. Somebody was badly needed for such a post, and from his record it might have been Conway; but Conway could not do it against the opposition of the Commander in Chief. Some other post, some command, must be found for him; for Washington was granitic and would never move. Conway, after all, still had his carefully cultivated friends in Congress and on the Board of War.

These latter, however, at the moment were in a state of

heartquake. Wilkinson, for instance. He had been appointed secretary to the Board of War, clearly a position of great strategic importance in the political war, the very day of his arrival in York with the long-awaited news. After some hesitation, and at the insistence of Horatio Gates, Congress had brevetted him a brigadier. He was only a tool, after all. Had he sat firm, and kept his mouth shut, he might have weathered the storm. But such behavior was not for James Wilkinson.

Vehemently he denied that he had ever said any such thing, though he confessed that he'd had a great deal to drink that night at Lord Stirling's. When Gates came down from Albany to take over the presidency of the Board of War, and, still trying to shake the blame onto somebody else, suggested that Wilkinson might have examined his private communications, Wilkinson flared, challenging.

Despite the difference in rank, such a meeting would be possible, since as members of the Board of War both were technically civilians. It did not take place immediately. Despite some confused and highly emotional negotiations, it was half a year later, near Harrison, New York, where both parties had gone to testify at the court martial proceedings against Brigadier Arthur St. Clair, that the men did at last meet with pistols.

Wilkinson was so touchy about his honor that men came to believe, correctly, that he had none. He demanded of Lord Stirling an explanation of his conduct that night in Reading. This he got, together with what amounted to an apology. He then demanded of Gates a letter attesting that he, Wilkinson, had behaved like a gentleman during the arrangements for the duel. Gates scorned to write any such paper; whereupon Wilkinson, in a pet, resigned from the army and from the Board of War.

Probably he believed that the resignation would not be accepted, and that with many a tut-tut he would be induced to remain, being indispensible. But the resignation *was* accepted. James Wilkinson was out.

He was a hard man to keep out. But when he did get back in, a year later, after a spell of real-estate speculation in and around Philadelphia, it was only as clothier general. In that post, at that time, his ability to hurt Washington was nil.

There were others, many others. Mifflin, for the moment, was abashed, and so was Gates; but William Whipple, Lovell, Reed, the Adamses, felt no obligation to be still. Conway too, though at last made to look the fool he was, kept his reputation as the best soldier, the best drillmaster, in America at that time; and he might yet be dangerous.

Washington, silent, sardonic, knew this. There was more to come; but he had won the first round.[49]

As for the boys on that cold hillside at Valley Forge, they hung on. After all, everything depended upon them.

Chapter Thirteen

THERE MUST have been times when they thought that the rest of the world had forgotten them, leaving them out there on that wind-swept slope, leaving them to die.

The battle with the weather always went on, but this had become instinctive. There was work, but it was dull work—drill, digging. No parties came from nearby towns, there being no nearby towns. Visitors were scattered, scared, and they called only on officers; while the private hitched his gaiters up and fastened his scarf a little tighter and went on shoveling, hoping as he did so that his fingers wouldn't freeze.

There had been several tries to induce farmers to set up a market within the limits of the camp; but farmers weren't interested. There simply was not enough trade.

Few wagons came, and few horses. Most of the higher officers, once the huts had been set up, quit the camp itself for more clubby quarters in farmhouses a few miles away. Their visits were routine, and as brief as they could make them. There was always a certain stir down at headquarters, but even that was far away, another world, literally outside the camp. The only horses *in* the camp were dead ones, skimpily buried when they were buried at all.

Birds didn't sing. What birds would there be? There were no herds of sheep or cows, no cackling flocks of geese or chickens to laugh at, to watch, even to study. As soon as any such creatures got into camp they were slaughtered. There was no time for fattening, no chance to make friends.

Neither sports nor games were organized. Who wanted to play in an icy rain, in a driving snow?

There were no parades to pick up pulses. Because of the clothing shortage it was seldom possible to get a whole company out at the same time, much less a regiment; for some had to stay back by the fire, shivering. Not infrequently the officers themselves, to the dismay of foreign observers, conducted their drills in dressing-robes.

Congress, on January 10, appointed a Committee of the Army (called the Committee of Conference), the purpose being to examine the camp and have talks with the Commander in Chief. These committeemen were in no sense busybodies and seemed anxious to help, but their presence meant little to the man who lugged a musket. They, for their part, were astounded by what they saw, and not a little disgusted too, and they quickly took up lodgings at the William Moore house two and a half miles north of camp. They observed off and on for about three months, and mostly they held their conferences at the Moore house or else at Washington's headquarters, only now and then, with a shudder, visiting the camp. The men didn't mind the visits. Even being stared at like so many animals in a zoo was better than being ignored.

The Committee of Conference at first consisted of Francis Dana, Joseph Reed, John Harvie, Nathaniel Folsom, and three members of the Board of War, Mifflin, Gates, and Pickering. The last three were excused from serving in view of their many other duties, and on January 20, Charles Carroll of Carrollton, Maryland, and Gouverneur Morris of New York were added. Carroll, the only Roman Catholic signer of the

Declaration of Independence, was the richest man in America; Morris was one of the wittiest. Carroll seems to have lingered but little at the Moore house;[50] but Morris, tiny, ebullient, young—he spent his twenty-sixth birthday, January 31, at the camp—was aghast at the conditions he found. "An army of skeletons appears before our eyes, naked, starved, sick, discouraged," he wrote to John Jay. From the first he not only supported Washington in all his plans, but did his brilliant best to bring the other committeemen into line.

"The Americans are bold, unyielding, and fearless . . . . they are by no means conquered," Baurmeister reported to his superior in Germany.[51] They would have liked to hear that.

Even those who surrounded them, it appeared, no longer liked them. Foraging never did make friends.

When it had become clear that the British would take Philadelphia, the more pronouncedly patriotic families there, those who could afford it, had made off to visit relatives or friends in the surrounding countryside, where they would be protected by Washington's ragged Continentals. For all this, the countryside, to the private at Valley Forge anyway, showed hostile. Despite patrols and penalties, the number of the "market people"—those who sneaked supplies into the city—increased. Farmers who saw the Continentals coming drove their livestock into the woods. Soon "siege conditions" in Philadelphia were no longer as severe as they had been early in the occupation period, though prices still were exceedingly high.

Pennsylvania, and particularly Bucks County, was "the enemy's country," in Pickering's phrase, and the common Continental soldier undoubtedly thought of the Quaker (whose numbers he exaggerated while he was unaware of their influence for good[52]) not as a neutral but as an opponent, a man to be watched.

The British paid in gold, while the value of Continental money went down and down, in part because of lack of confidence in Congress and the army, in part because the British had brought printing presses over on various vessels and were flooding the country with counterfeit Continental bills—the first time this weapon had been used.[53]

Congress had granted Washington for a limited time extraordinary powers of seizure, and recently, just before the move to Valley Forge, these powers had been renewed, though not at his request. He was reluctant to use them. He knew the suspicion with which Americans viewed any standing army, any show of organized martial force, and his foraging parties had orders to pay for everything with paper money ("If Congress needs rags to make paper with we've got plenty of them," the boys at camp said) and not to be rough. Perhaps these orders were not always interpreted by the letter. "Harden your heart," General Greene told one foraging officer. "We are in the midst of a damned nest of Tories."[54]

The dangerous enemy was not the British army but indifference.

"I am tired of the languor with which so sacred a war as this is carried on," John Laurens of the headquarters staff at Valley Forge wrote to his father.[55] The trouble was, few except the most ardent in the field thought of the war as "sacred." Many did not think of it at all. This fact never failed to astonish foreigners, for each landed on these shores expecting to find them in a ferment. "There is a hundred times more enthusiasm for this Revolution in the first café you choose to name at Paris than there is in all the United States together," Du Portail, the French chief of engineers at Valley Forge, wrote to a friend.[56]

Separate states might become officially aware of the war at intervals, when it got near; but their efforts were spasmodic, not sustained.

At Valley Forge, at the blackest of all times, this was the men's blackest thought: that so many fellow Americans had forgotten them.

Chapter Fourteen

THERE WAS another person who forgot the Continentals, and the Continentals were glad of it. This was Sir William Howe.

He lolled. By the side of Mrs. Loring, indolently waving or touching his hat to acquaintances, he rode forth in his carriage for a little air; or he sat at dinner or, more often, at the gaming table. He spent many hours horizontally. "If we could only get him out of his bed and onto his horse," staff officers used to cry.

Those were good days in Philadelphia, despite the siege, for the large Whig exodus before the occupation had left convenient quarters, and the city was not overcrowded.

The siege did have its awkward aspects, granted. There was the matter of firewood.

The supply ships could bring almost everything into Philadelphia, convoyed as they were by Admiral Howe's war vessels —though thanks to the activities of American privateers, even the convoyed insurance rates had doubled, while those for unconvoyed vessels had gone to six times what they were before the war, according to the register of the Society of Merchants

Sir William Howe. *Courtesy New York Public Library Picture Collection*

(Lloyd's), London, and seamen's wages had risen from twenty-five to fifty-five shillings a month—but they could hardly be expected to bring firewood, of which they themselves often stood in need on arrival.

As England itself had been only a little while before, eastern America was heavily wooded. The woods, however, did not cluster around the city, as Continental outposts did. An enormous amount of fuel was needed every day to take care of army, navy, and civilian population, and since most of it came from private parks, and since the British too were making a fairly serious effort to pay for everything they took, it cost a lot of money. The lack of it from time to time caused a certain amount of—well, not suffering as they knew suffering out at Valley Forge, but inconvenience.

General Baurmeister complained in a letter home that he was obliged to buy three-eighths of a cord of wood a week in order to keep his fireplace going, at five shillings a cord *gold*. He added, though, that at least they were being issued "rum of the best quality."[57]

There was another thing that the British army rather painfully wanted, and at this juncture could do little about. That was flints. Or rather, good flints.

In a war in which it was said that it took a man's weight in bullets to kill him, there was a great deal of shooting. Lead was plentiful in the British army, and powder and steel, but not flints. Every time a striker fell, even if there was no explosion, the flint was chipped when it struck the steel. This could happen sixty times and more with the high-grade black flints the Continentals used—it was one of the few evidences of their preparedness—but a British musketeer who got half of that from his flint was lucky. Some of the flints could be resharpened, though not under battle conditions. The British, like the Continentals, used a wooden "driver" or "snapper," a dummy flint, for reloading practice—which practice involved twelve separate motions with their brown Bess—but these would be thrown away when trouble loomed. So they did envy the Continentals at least their flints.

For the rest, they were cozy enough in Philadelphia, and if Mrs. Loring could lose three hundred guineas in one night, that hurt only her—and Howe. They even had some luxuries: green turtle from the Bahamas, claret and Madeira from Spain. The drinks and food at the Bunch of Grapes or the Indian Queen were good. The officers, a large number of whom were rich and titled, put on a ball every week at Smith's City Tavern in Second Street. And there was the cockpit in Moore's Alley.

There was also the theater on the south side of South Street, near Fourth, a location which at that time was just outside the city limits. The theater was built there for the same reason that most Elizabethan theaters were across the Thames in Southwark—to evade puritanical city ordinances. There, with the talented and amiable young Major André[58] painting many of the scenes and writing not a few of the lines as well, the officers put on *The Minor, The Deuce is in Him, Duke and No Duke, The Constant Couple, The Mock Doctor,*—plays that could hardly be called heavy, but it passed the time.

When the weather moderated a bit there was also, of course, cricket. Philadelphia took to cricket.[59]

There were unfortunate incidents, but not many of them. Now and then one of the perfumed dandies went a bit too far, jarring a public by no means priggish; but on the whole the civilians, if they didn't cheer, at least did not catcall either. And the females among them habitually fluttered when in the presence of the foe. There was even an expression to describe falling in love with a redcoat: it was called catching scarlet fever.

Through it all, virtually nothing was done about the conflict. Local enlistments had been disappointing, barely three hundred. And Howe loafed. Easygoing, no martinet, Howe was popular with his men; yet there were those who fretted, and some even apostrophized him in verse:

> "Awake, arouse, Sir Billy.
> There's forage in the plain.
> Ah! leave your little Filly,

And open the campaign.
Heed not a woman's prattle,
Which tickles in the ear,
But give the word for battle,
And grasp the warlike spear."

Sir William grasped no spear. He did not even get out of bed. Why should he? It was warm in there.

Chapter Fifteen

DIARISTS ARE unaccountable. They were many, for diaries were the fashion then—and they came from all ranks. Some of their efforts were thoughtful, some trite, a few funny. For the most part they were terse. This could hardly have been because the diarists were kept so busy. More likely the cold accounts for it, or a shortage of ink. (On January 15, Washington, out of sealing wax, wrote to General Heath to get him some in Boston; and on February 27, he even had to write to the Board of War —the Commander in Chief himself!—to complain about a lack of writing paper.) Entries, in any event, tended to be laconic. Albigence Waldo, for example, could write "Provisions Scarce" one day, "Snow'd all day" the next; though now and then, as on December 22, he might wax savage: "The Lord send that our Commissary of Purchases may live [on] Fire Cake & Water, 'till their glutted Gutts are turned to Pasteboard."

The humor was largely unconscious. A classic bit is that of Private David How, who thus describes the most famous of all American crossings: "25 This Day at 12 aClock we march[d] Down the River about 12 miles. in the Night we Crossed the River Dullerway [Delaware] With a large Body of men and Field Pieces. 26 This morning at 4 aClock We got off with our

Field pieces Marchd 8 miles to Trenton Whare we ware Atacked by a Number of Hushing [Hessians] & we Toock 1000 of them besides killed Some Then we march[d] back And got to the River at Night and got over all the Hushing."[60]

Sometimes the note might be merry. Like Waldo, James Thacher was a surgeon. When he addressed himself to his diary he could be chatty, even bright. February 4, for example:

"Several gentlemen belonging to the hospital being desireous of improving in the accomplishment of dancing, Mr. John Trotter has agreed to open a special school for our accomoda- tion and we are to attend every afternoon. Master Trotter has for many years been in the practice of teaching the art in New York, and has acquired great fame as a man of knowledge and experience in his profession. He is about fifty eight years of age, a small, genteel, well proportioned man. . . . Under the tuition of such a master, we flatter ourselves that in due time, if we improve our advantages, we shall be able to figure in a ball room."

Thacher's hospital, however, was at Albany, where after the surrender of Burgoyne there were many British and Hessian surgeons to assist the local staff. No Trotters taught their art at Valley Forge.

There was a shortage of medicines, but there had always been that. What was graver was the shortage of soap. Once again the commissary had broken down. There were supposed to be three ounces of soft soap or one ounce of hard soap is- sued to every man every week for clothes, quarters, and person. This was scanty enough, but it was not always there.

Valley Forge was no dirtier than any other camp. The usual precautions were taken, the usual latrines dug. There was precious little garbage to dispose of anyway, though admittedly the corpses of starved horses did present a problem. The climate, if severe, was healthful. The diet, though limited, at least wasn't fattening. There were no springs in that high rocky place, and to get water it was necessary to go down to the Schuylkill on the north or the Valley Creek on the west, or else to go to a brook about half a mile south of the camp. The brook was most often used, with the result that its water, roiled, was muddy all day.

If the men had been given enough soap they would have been better soldiers. Though perhaps they were by nature slovenly, as foreigners charged, it is certain that they would have preferred to be clean; but you can't get rid of lice just by cursing them, and fleas, too, ignore regulations.

The anomalous position of the surgeon did not help. He was neither officer nor enlisted man. Though educated, he had little authority, and his so-called "mates" as often as not were mere misfits, men the colonel didn't know what else to do with.

In his monumental report of January 28 to the Congressional committee investigating the army, George Washington had little to say about what would today be called the medical corps, and it is clear that it did not interest him. He did point out that there was bickering and name-calling between the regimental surgeons inside camp and the hospital surgeons outside. The hospital men cried that by the time they got the patient he was at least half dead thanks to the mishandling of the surgeons in camp, who countered with the allegation that the hospital surgeons were given all the good medicines and equipment, and that they, the regimental men, seldom had any chance to effect a cure. Washington found this deplorable, but he had no suggestions to make.

It might be thought that after two major battles, each a defeat, the Continental army would contain a large number of surgical cases, men recovering from wounds. This was not the case.

Though the military musket of the day wouldn't shoot far and surely wouldn't shoot straight, it did discharge a deadly missile. The balls, each weighing about an ounce, had a terrific stopping power. A man hit with one went right over backward, usually with a few smashed bones. Moreover, these balls were made by squeezing heated lead into a mould consisting of two pincered hemispheres. At the junction of those hemispheres, like an equator, inevitably there was left a ridged seam. The effect on striking was much like that of a modern dumdum bullet. The ball *tore,* it *ripped,* inflicting a larger, messier hole than might have been expected, a wound not likely to heal. Only very strong men, or the lucky ones, recovered; and most of those were amputees of no further value to the army.

Not the enemy with the red coat, then, but that older, deadlier enemy, disease, was what filled the hospitals of the Continental army. There was a great deal of dysentery, and that most terrible of all killers, typhus, strode abroad.

In the camp itself there was no more than a medical station, a first-aid post. The sick, and such wounded as there were, were taken to improvised hospitals in the neighborhood. The largest of these was at Yellow Springs, eight miles west of the forks of Pickering Creek, where the water was deeply tinted with iron. This was thought of as a health resort, "the Bath of America," and until the war it had been fashionable. The building, a three-story one, was large, one hundred feet by thirty-six, and had wide verandas. More than thirteen hundred were treated there in all.

There were smaller places, usually farmhouses, at Princeton, Burlington, Trenton, Reading, Allentown, Trappe, Easton, Manheim. The soldiers sometimes cursed the Quakers for their refusal to bear arms, for the soldiers believed in the old adage "Whoever ain't for me is agin me"; but the Quakers did noble work in tending the sick, and so did the members of certain other pacifistic Pennsylvania sects. At Ephrata, for instance, forty miles west of Valley Forge, the Spiritual Virgins toiled tirelessly; the Moravians served at Lititz and at Bethlehem, a town with a population of about five hundred which was doubled by the sick from camp.

Each of these places was understaffed, and so a pest house. There were not enough blankets, and almost no beds. The dead and the dying lay side by side. Four or five men might die successively on a given portion of the floor before the overworked nurse could get around to changing the straw.

A general order of about this time[61] provided that each hospital be visited by a field officer regularly—once a day when possible, in any event not less than twice a week—and set forth ten responsibilities, things to watch for. These were not medical but disciplinary, and included an outlook for malingering, the checking of equipment and arms of arriving and departing patients, the disposal and record of dead bodies, policing of the whole place, etc. These were reforms, and as far as they went good; but they got nowhere near the root of the problem.

A single statistic: of forty men from Gibson's Sixth Virginia Regiment hospitalized at Bethlehem, three survived. A staff sergeant there averred that twenty patients died of "camp diseases" to every one who died by "weapons of the enemy."[62]

This was not bad. In the days when typhus cut down hosts as never Attila could, or Tamerlane or Genghis Khan, when whole crusades were wiped out by the flea that the rat carries,[63] the percentage would have been much greater; and even in the latest war, the one before this, the so-called Seven Years War of Europe, Great Britain lost 1,512 men in action, 134,000 in hospitals.[64]

The Continentals of the winter 1777-78 might not have been prepossessing, and certainly they weren't trim; but they were hardy.

Chapter Sixteen

THERE WAS a great deal of digging to be done.

Much has been made of the fact that most members of the Continental army before their enlistment were familiar with firearms. It could be added as a point of equal importance that many, being farmers or frontiersmen, were skilled as well with ax and shovel. The redcoats in scorn called them "diggers"; but the Continentals made no bones about their conviction that a trench is a good thing to have when there's a chance that somebody will shoot at you—and the same could be said of a breastwork.

Valley Forge was naturally a strong defensive position. Omitting outposts, the camp proper extended about nine miles along the top of the ridge.

To the north and northwest, forming about half of the perimeter on the side away from Philadelphia, ran the Schuylkill. Between Washington's advance post at Matson's Ford (now Conshohocken) and the rear guard at the present town of Phoenixville, there were six fords. Only one of these, however, the Fatland Ford, led to the camp itself. This front, if front it could be called, was deemed so hard of access, at least from Philadelphia, that it was guarded only by a few scattered pickets and, in the center, a large fort, the largest in camp, called the Star Redoubt. Stirling's men and Washington's headquarters were at the extreme western end, and except for the Commander in Chief's bodyguard, which was made up of Virginians, and McIntosh's Georgians nearby, the line was held almost entirely by New Englanders—Sullivan's New Hampshirites at the ford itself, while Rhode Island and Connecticut men under Varnum manned the Star Redoubt.

The west was covered by the Valley Creek, flowing in a deep gorge between Mount Misery and the slope of the camp itself, a place where it would have been hard to deploy many troops

Valley Forge—Stirling Redoubt showing General Knox's Artillery. *Courtesy Valley Forge State Park Commission*

for an assault. Nevertheless the top of the ridge at that point was protected by a trench, earthen breastworks, and a palisade made of crisscrossed horizontal logs, with here and there an outjutting redan.

Similar, though even stronger fortifications were built on the edge of the ridge along the southern and southeastern front, the side of Philadelphia, the only side from which a massive attack could with reason be expected. The ground below this position was bare and level for a long way, and cannons mounted in forts at either end of the line could break up any massing of assault troops there, using canister that would carry four times as far as a musket ball.

This southern front was strongly manned, nine brigades being stationed there—from west to east, Woodford's, Scott's, Wayne's, Poor's, Glover's, Learned's, Paterson's, Weedon's, and Muhlenberg's.

Even if an enemy somehow should storm this line, and break through, he would find himself on the high, wide, level parade, enfiladed from both sides by "forts" that were in fact fortified gun emplacements, and faced by an inner line of trenches and

Valley Forge—Inner Line Rifle Pit. *Courtesy Valley Forge State Park Commission*

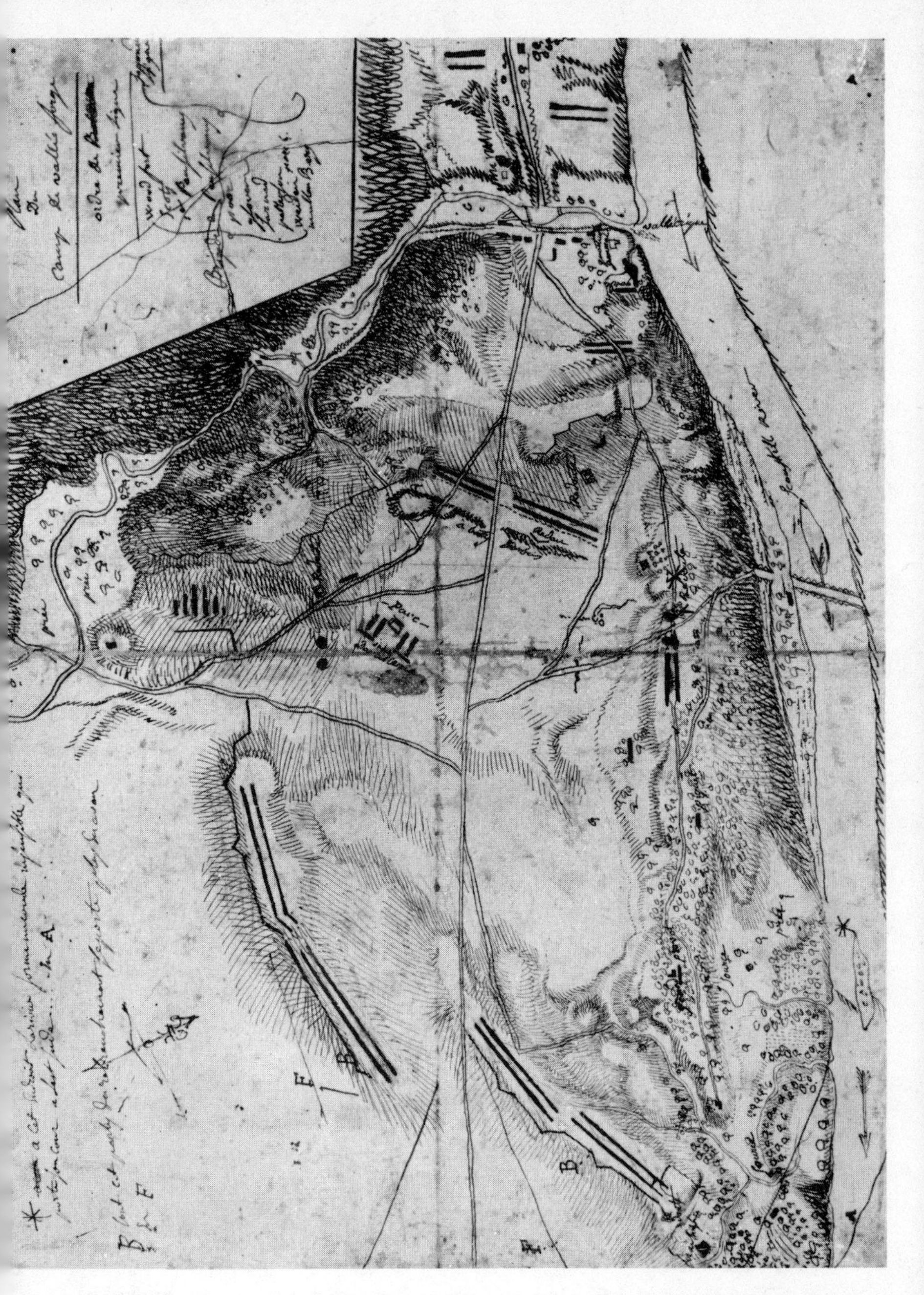

Du Portail's Map of Valley Forge. *Courtesy The Historical Society of Pennsylvania*

a stout abatis made of fallen trees, the branches of which, toward the enemy, had been spike-sharpened.

The chopping down of trees for the abatis and for the breastworks, following upon the chopping for the huts, had left the top of Valley Forge as bald as an egg. There would be no cover there.

However, this was not done in a day, nor yet in a week. The men were got indoors first, the huts built. Breastworks had to wait. It was spring before they were finished. If Howe had moved against the camp at Valley Forge at any time before that, the story might have had a different ending.

". . . the present newly adopted encampment, Gen. du Portail assures me," Henry Laurens wrote to James Duane, April 7,[65] "is tenable against the Enemy's utmost effort by their present powers."

If Du Portail had said that, it was so. He was not a man to make mistakes.

Brigadier General Louis Le Bègue de Presle du Portail, chevalier of France, later to become a marshal and minister of war, was dour and sour. He was haughty in his manner and opinionated. Neither his fellow officers nor the men who took orders from him liked the man. But he knew his business. A military engineer, he had a handful of military engineers to work with, his fellow countrymen; and they got things done.[66]

The Continental cause was fortunate when Du Portail and his little band of workers volunteered.

Chapter Seventeen

It was a Sunday morning in January, 1776, at Woodstock, Virginia, and the pastor had taken for his text the third chapter of Ecclesiastes.

"To every thing there is a season, and a time to every purpose under the heaven . . . a time to weep and a time to laugh; a time to get and a time to lose . . . a time to keep silence and a time to speak."

He added that there was also a time to pray and a time to fight.

Whereupon he took off his clerical robe to exhibit himself in the uniform of a colonel of militia, and left the pulpit and strode outside, where he called for recruits.

Born at Trappe, Pennsylvania, John Peter Gabriel Muhlenberg as a young man was sent back to the old country to study for the church. Even as ministers' sons go, he seems to have been frisky. "Teufel Piet" fellow students called him. When he returned, later settling in Virginia, it was to learn that he could not practice his profession—or at least expect to make a living out of it—unless he was an Anglican priest. Such was the grip that the Church of England, more royal than the King, had upon the colonies. Moreover, there was no bishop on this side of the sea to lay hands on him; for despite many an excuse—to the colonists it seemed an attitude of ecclesiastical arrogance—the Church had not seen fit to create an American see. For reasons lost to memory, the thirteen colonies were included in the See of London, though no Bishop of London or any other bishop ever had deigned to visit them. (Spain, less stingy, at this time had seven archbishops and forty-one bishops in Latin America;[67] but that was of course the Roman Catholic Church.)

Not easily daunted, young Muhlenberg went to England, where he studied for another year and became a priest, presumably an Anglo-Lutheran. He returned to the colonies, preached in several New Jersey parishes, then accepted a call to Woodstock where, in 1775, when war was brewing, he organized the Eighth (German) Virginia Regiment, of which he was colonel.

The pastor had made no secret of his martial activities. Though it was a dramatic act when he peeled off that robe, it could hardly have astounded his parishioners. He meant it when he said that this was a time to fight. Made a brigadier in the field a year later, he was no summer soldier; for he was in the thick of it at the Brandywine and at Germantown, and he was with the army throughout the terrible winter of Valley Forge, always ready with a fist or a psalm, his headquarters in the northeastern corner of camp, his voice at council invariably raised for the bold course.

Muhlenberg was the highest-ranking clergyman in the Continental army, but he was by no means the only one. They ranged from privates to majors, and of course many were chaplains.

The position of the chaplain was anomalous. Whether he was paid, and if so how much—indeed whether he could even be there—depended in large part upon the colonels or upon the soldiers themselves. This was especially true of the New England troops, whose spiritual leaders were their own, and personally acceptable, not assigned from the outside. Some, conscious of home ties, came and went. Others, like David Avery of Gageborough, Massachusetts, stayed all winter.

Stories about pastors of the Muhlenberg type were without number, especially in New England. Preachers would go to church with a musket in one hand, a Bible in the other. They recruited companies. They marched, and in many cases fought.

It could be supposed that the men of Valley Forge, so sorely tried, would turn to thoughts of God as the desert traveler to water. Perhaps many did, but not in public. There were Sunday services; but there was no steady, over-all church organization, and there was no outstanding preacher. There was no point-at-able *policy* with regard to religion. Washington himself, a reticent man in this as in so many other respects, was not one to set an example; for though he himself was an Anglican, clearly he believed that a man's religious beliefs were his own business. Washington went to church from time to time, and after his wife came to camp he went every Sunday; but he never did stay, as she used to do, to take Communion.[68]

The amazing thing about the camp was not that there seemed

to be so little formal religion in it, but that religious differences, all winter, led to no trouble.

For those differences were real. They weren't forced; they were not the pets of fanatics.

The country could be said to be divided, religiously, into three parts.

In New England the Congregationalists outnumbered the Presbyterians, and the Presbyterians by far outnumbered those of any other denomination. Often it was difficult to tell Congregationalists and Presbyterians apart; and the average scoffing Southerner did not attempt to do so, classing them all as Presbyterian. In any event the puritans had no use for the Church of England with its censers, candles, and silk robes, smacking of Rome. They pointed out, with a persistence that could have been exasperating, that most of the Tory intellectuals in the colonies, the pamphleteers and important loyalist orators—Samuel Seabury, Miles Cooper, Samuel Peters, Samuel Auchmuty, Charles Inglis, Thomas Bradbury Chandler, Jonathan Boucher—were Anglican divines.

The Church of England was represented in every colony, but only in the South was it accepted as "official." The Southerners looked upon the "leveling" tactics of New Englanders, the "saints," the "wise men of the East," not with disgust merely but with alarm. If the whole new nation was to be made as democratic as that, what were we coming to, what were we fighting for?

With one spot excepted, only in the middle states was there any toleration. Pennsylvania was the most liberal of all, even more so, in respect of Roman Catholicism, than Maryland. Quakers and other pacifistic groups abounded in Pennsylvania. Southerners and New Englanders alike looked upon this as a perilous position to take.

The exception was Rhode Island, where Baptists were tolerated, even Jews. Rhode Islanders on occasion could go yet further. When Major General Greene appointed a *Universalist,* John Murray, as chaplain of one of his Rhode Island regiments, every chaplain at Valley Forge protested. Greene was having trouble with his eyes at the time, but he could always see his duty. He stuck by Murray, who stayed.[69]

Chapter Eighteen

GEORGE WASHINGTON "is the most kindly, most obliging, and most liberal man, but as a general he is too slow, even lazy, much too weak, and not without his dose of vanity and presumption. My opinion is that if he does anything sensational he will owe it more to his good luck or to his adversary's mistakes than to his own ability."

Thus Johann Kalb wrote to his patron, the Comte de Broglie, September 24, 1777, shortly after he arrived in this country.

"He has not yet overcome his old prejudice against the French," the writer added.[70]

One of Washington's most significant qualities is not mentioned, perhaps because, rare anywhere, it was almost unknown among European generals of the time. *He could learn by his mistakes.* The man whom Kalb had met, if briefly, at the time he dashed off this report, and the man who led the tatterdemalion Continental forces from the Gulph to Valley Forge, were two different persons, the latter much greater than the first. Washington, under pressure, grew as you watched him.

As for the "prejudice," perhaps Kalb picked the wrong word there. Certainly, and not without reason, Washington *disliked* Frenchmen.

Save for a trip to the West Indies as a lad turning twenty, he had not traveled. He knew no word of French, a fact that could have made him self-conscious when he came among cosmopolites. But there was more to it.

Some in the patriot cause argued that no cynical monarchy like France ever did anything from disinterested motives. That Vergennes, the foreign minister, that dry, industrious man, that stick, already was eying Canada, from which France could easily dominate the coastal states; and that to go from the tyranny of England to that of France would be to jump from the frying pan into the fire.

The overwhelming majority, however, thought France our best chance. Clearly some foreign alliance was needed: there never had been a thought of winning independence unaided. Spain had been hoped for, and still might come into the fray under the terms of its no-Pyrenees pact with France; but Spain, already rotten, was fearful for Florida, and would not view with joy the emergence of a new and powerful republic in America. The Netherlands too were a possibility; but if they did come in it would be only on the sea, and there was danger that their price might be at least a renewed foothold in New York, the erstwhile New Amsterdam, which would of course split the just-born nation in half.

France had a vast reserve of experienced soldiers. She had of late built up her navy. She teetered on the verge of bankruptcy, true; but her hatred of England was such that she might well be swept into the fight.

We had many friends in France. The boldness of our stand against the biggest empire in history at the peak of its power was applauded by many, watched with interest by all. Republican ideas were popular in Louis XVI's realm; and if they were somewhat different from the republican ideas entertained on this side of the Atlantic, the difference was not immediately apparent to Frenchmen, who felt a surge of sympathy for the American colonists.

Vergennes, the chief minister, was a cautious man, methodical, proper, a titled clerk; but with a hand held behind his back he could sometimes pass out supplies. Totally different was his tool, that exuberant, flamboyant, utterly unpredictable harp teacher, watchmaker and theorist, Beaumarchais, the King's friend, author of *The Barber of Seville,* who had set up business as Rodrique Hortalez et Cie in the enormous Hôtel de Hollande, Faubourg du Temple, from where with a few million livres contributed from time to time by France and Spain he was shipping all sorts of things to the states. This was strictly unofficial. Spain—France too—denied all knowledge of it.

These goods were good. The uniforms were of fine cloth and well tailored. The bayonets, so badly needed, were long and sharp. The muskets were excellent, much better than the average of our own, in the opinion of many experts even better than the British brown Bess.

Unfortunately the men France had been sending were not all as good as the muskets. This was in large part our own fault; for Arthur Lee and Silas Deane, neither of whom would believe anything the other said, believed whatever was told to them, through an interpreter, by the most improbable adventurers whom they signed up by the score, promising them high rank.

Now, the new army undoubtedly needed engineers, as it needed artillerymen. There was no *background* for engineering here. What little had been done in the past had been done by the military themselves, the redcoats, so that our own citizens had been wont to look on such work as bridge-building, demolition, and the construction of a Vauban wall as they looked on the manual of arms: an activity for slaves, a practice associated with that most hated of all institutions, the standing army. Our officers had to learn those things right from books.

Some of the Frenchmen who soon began to descend upon America might have been good engineers and artillerymen. A few might even have been half as good as they said they were. But for the most part they couldn't speak English; they were disgusted with the appearance and manners of the Americans and didn't hesitate to say so; they were out for money, money; and they demanded high ranks.

Most of them bore letters promising the said ranks; but not all of those letters were from Silas Deane, though many were. The French West Indies since the end of the Seven Years War had been filled with ex-officers who, thrown out of work, had sought a fortune in planting—and failed to find it. Many of these men were aristocrats, but that didn't deter them from wrapping themselves in a republican mantle at the arrival of news of hostilities on the mainland, and offering their skill and experience, and incidentally their lives, to the glorious cause of freedom. In a raw provincial horde like the Continental army they would of course all rate as generals, with appropriate pay. These men—and there were hundreds of them—got letters of recommendation from their colonial governors, who in many cases were glad to get rid of them; and when they landed in quest of glory such letters were all they did have. Some got no farther than Charleston, South Carolina, which thereupon developed a French quarter.

Philadelphia too had been filled with them—arrogant, penniless, disdainful, stiff. Thomas Conway was among the first.

Among the first also had been Tronson du Coudrai, one of the Duc de Choiseul's men (the Duc was out of power and trying to get back) and an engineer of some standing, though his military experience was not great. He was personally obnoxious, haughty, pompous; but it would have been hard to repudiate that letter from Silas Deane, a letter that assured him, more or less, the moon. Du Coudrai not only insisted upon high places for all his followers, but stated that he himself must be made a major general and put in complete command of all artillery and engineering.

Congress paused, abashed. And George Washington stepped in.

Washington tried to be fair. He did not despise all Frenchmen. Nathanael Greene thought them "so many spies in our camp,"[71] but Washington saw merit in many, who served us faithfully and well, filling a void. Washington considered Colonel de la Radière, for instance, "a Man who understands his profession,"[72] and he had the liveliest admiration for Du Portail. But when Henry Knox, the Continental army's head of artillery and one of Washington's closest advisers, threatened to resign if a foreigner was put over him, and two trusted major generals, like Knox enormously popular in the army and invaluable in council—John Sullivan and Nathanael Greene—intimated that they would resign if Knox did, then Washington was obliged to take action. He spoke up.

On the other hand, it would not do to step on too many French toes. Théveneau de Francy had come to this country as Beaumarchais's representative, and if certain persons in Paris were rubbed the wrong way that life-giving gush of matériel from the old Dutch embassy in the Faubourg du Temple might dry up. All the newcomers claimed to be close to everybody of importance in France from the King down; and at that stage of the war, and at that distance, nobody here was sure how much truth there might be in those claims.

The matter of Du Coudrai at last was settled by making him a major general, and his hangers-on for the most part colonels, but keeping Henry Knox as chief of artillery. Du Coudrai's title was to be inspector general of ordnance and military manufactory. In that office he might have caused much harm had he lived a little longer. He was on his way to join the army on the Brandywine when, crossing the Schuylkill on a ferry, though warned, he refused to dismount. The crossing was rough. The horse was frightened, and bolted—overboard. Horse and rider alike were drowned; and it was a good horse.

But Washington had been warned, as had Congress. The office of inspector general of ordnance and military manufactory remained vacant, and Frenchmen thereafter were scrutinized with care.

Chapter Nineteen

Baron de Kalb was not entitled to the title, any more than he was entitled to the "de." He was born Johann Kalb, of Hüttendorf peasants. Going into the army, he did well, married money, rose. He was middle-aged when he came to America with Lafayette, and most of his service had been in the French army, where in the elite regiments it was impossible to become an officer *without* a title; so he had taken one.

He was testy, crusty, no genius, but a hard worker. He spoke English, having visited these shores once before. If the letter quoted in the previous chapter would seem to suggest that he was lacking in judgment, it should be explained that he had a special reason for belittling Washington to the Comte de Broglie. He wished to let the Count down easily.

Though he had risen high, Kalb yet needed a patron, as was the custom of the time. The Comte de Broglie was a younger brother of the Duc de Broglie, a marshal of France and one of the few French military leaders who had emerged from the Seven Years War with an enhanced reputation. The Count was not a marshal, and his military and diplomatic experience alike seem to have been scanty, in some cases even a bit shady.

He was a tiny man, but his ideas were big. He was prepared to consent to become the dictator of America, provided that certain conditions were met.

On December 17, 1776, Silas Deane, in Paris, had received a letter. It had been written by Kalb but beyond all doubt inspired by the Comte de Broglie, who at that time was at his country seat near Ruffec, and unemployed.

This amazing letter, which must have had official sanction,[73] started by comparing the new American republic to Holland, which had found in William of Orange its stadholder—and savior. It acknowledged France's interest in the present struggle. Then, with a straight face, it asserted that "what is necessary for these States, now in the position of mere children, is some foreign troops, and especially a commander of high reputation in Europe,—one who . . . should unite a name made illustrious by many heroes to a long military experience."

Such a commander, the letter continued, without explaining how this figure had been reached, would be worth twenty thousand troops.

If it be objected that this smacked of despotism, the very thing the colonies were fighting to escape, Kalb went on, his answer was that this great European leader would have in America military control only. And if to that it was further objected that he who has supreme military control not infrequently finds it easy to gain supreme political control, Kalb would beg to point out that the "noble and generous heart" of this exalted personage, whose name is never mentioned, "would be incapable of anything of the kind."

Finally, the Americans should ask for the services of this paragon, rather than have the deal started the other way round, and at the same time, and in order to enhance his dignity, they should request of Louis XVI (the only mention of nationality) that he first be created a duke and made a marshal.

De Broglie followed this with a letter of his own, coming right out in the open and admitting that he was putting himself forward as the dictator in question. He said that he would serve for no longer than three years, and added as an afterthought that besides the supreme military command he should be given the exclusive power to conduct all negotiations between the United States and foreign countries.

Today this proposal seems preposterous, an egregious burst of vanity. Yet it was put forward in all seriousness; and as politico-military thinking went at that time, it was sensible and even sound.

It just didn't allow for the feelings of the Americans.

There is not in either letter anything to indicate that De Broglie had the slightest knowledge of or interest in the principles for which the colonists were fighting.

Published, this correspondence might have caused a break in relations and a different end of the American Revolution; but Benjamin Franklin came to Paris at about this time, inserting a little sense into our mission, and the matter was quietly dropped.

Nevertheless it is likely—all but certain—that when at last Kalb had managed to arrange to go to America as a member of the Lafayette group, he carried some such letter from the Comte de Broglie, who still had his hopes.

These hopes were dashed by Kalb, who after one look around

The Marquis de Lafayette. *Courtesy New York Public Library Picture Collection*

knew that his patron would do well to stay home. Kalb was tactful about this, and a judicious belittling of George Washington might offer De Broglie some balm.

Kalb could have been nettled too by the way the Lafayette party was received.

Marie Joseph Paul Yves Roch Gilbert du Motier, Marquis de Lafayette, who a few months before had scarcely even heard of America, had paid for his own passage in a chartered ship, and his party included sundry soldiers of rank, among whom Kalb was easily the senior. They landed at Charleston after an eventful voyage, having dodged British warships. Undergoing great hardships, most of the way on foot, they traveled overland to Philadelphia, where on the morning of July 28, 1777, washed and brushed, they presented themselves before the door of Congress.

They were told, harshly and in very bad French, that they were not wanted. Then the door was closed, leaving them out in the street.

Lafayette was nineteen years old. He stood five feet nine, and had high-humped shoulders. He was earnest, ambitious, by no means good-looking—sandy hair, fine hazel eyes, a long, high, craggy nose—and very rich.

He was without wit, and today it almost seems without wits. Yet there was something about him . . . His celebrated boyishness, which was to become rather shopworn, at this time still was fresh. There could be no question about his physical courage, and he did have an aptitude for army life. He was said to be well connected at court, and never denied this. He had left a girl-wife, beautiful but pregnant, and an infant daughter, in France. He had inherited 130,000 livres—or 14,000 pounds—a year, and he wasn't afraid of spending it. If he was a trifle hazy as to what the war was all about, he was perfectly clear concerning the part he himself wanted to play: he wanted to be right in the front of every action, waving a sword.

After his rebuff he retired to his inn and wrote a letter to Congress, relating that he had come a long way to help the American cause and that he asked no salary and would pay all his own expenses.

This brought a more civil answer. Congress fell to thinking about it. A Frenchman who paid his own way was a novelty. They made him a major general.

Then he met Washington, who was kind. To Washington politeness to a stranger of gentle birth was natural, not an imposed duty; yet it is sure that he went out of his way in the case of "Fayette," as he always thought of this youngster.[74] He invited him to visit the camp, then about five miles north of Philadelphia, between Germantown and the Schuylkill. At the first staff conference he pointedly asked Lafayette's opinion. It was Lafayette whom he invited to ride by his side in that August 24 parade through Philadelphia; and when Lafayette was wounded in the leg at the Brandywine, where he fought well, the Commander in Chief over some weeks inquired thoughtfully and often about his condition. Indeed, Washington took an instant liking to this gay erratic lad, who from the first adored him.

Washington had no children. It has been sometimes said that he refused to give Lafayette a field command because he feared that the youngster might be killed. This was not Washington's way. It is much more likely that he interpreted the action of Congress in making Lafayette a major general as a gesture of friendliness toward France, not as an order to hand the lad a division to play with. He could love him without trusting his discretion.

Whatever the reason, he *did* love him. And this was the reason why his heart sank when, on January 23, in one of the darkest of times at Valley Forge, Lafayette, having just come from York, displayed the Board of War's command to head an expedition into Canada.

They were trying to split them! That must have been Washington's thought.

Thomas Conway, who had toadied to Lafayette, begging the Marquis to deem him "his soldier," was to be second in command.

Washington read the order through, then handed it back without a word. He was a busy man, and this was not the first time that he had been hit an unfair blow; but it did hurt.

Chapter Twenty

LAFAYETTE DID not fare well on the "iruption into Canada." His imagination soaring, he had paused only long enough, after getting his orders, to inform the Board of War in no uncertain tones that he meant to report directly to his Commander in Chief, George Washington, and to send to sundry relatives and friends at home a batch of letters in which he described himself, the knight in shining armor, as about to win Canada back to the lilies of France. Then he galloped north.

He had been promised twenty-five hundred troops, but at Albany he found fewer than half this number, many of them sick. Brigadier John Stark had been supposed to join him with his Green Mountain Boys, but Stark, it turned out, had no orders—and virtually no men. The commissary, ordinarily a strong one despite the regulations with which it was shackled (Washington had tried in vain to get Congress to transfer to Valley Forge one or both of its deputies, Udny Hay and Henry Emanuel Lutterloh), at the moment was in sad condition. There were no funds. There was very little ammunition. The British, aware that another invasion was planned, were massing to meet it; and scouts reported that they were much stronger than had at first been thought.

The thing looked impossible. Lincoln, Arnold, Schuyler, even Conway, advised against trying it.

Lafayette wept. He wrote wild letters. He spent a great deal of his own money. He proposed a descent upon New York City, a harebrained scheme soon dropped. He raged.

One thing at least was certain: for this particular fiasco the Commander in Chief could not be blamed. Whether through carelessness or a deliberate effort to snub Washington, the Board of War had not even mentioned this "iruption" to him.[75] Yet these same men, and a good part of Congress as well, were embarrassed and even distressed by the young Frenchman's vexation. Lafayette could not forget those perfervid letters that predicted miracles, himself the magician with the wand. He would be made to seem a fool before everybody who counted! His screams were loud, reaching from Albany, New York, to York, Pennsylvania. He squealed that he was the victim of a plot. What if, in a fury, he quit the country, refusing to play any more? What would the rest of the world think? Would those supplies keep coming in from Rodrique Hortalez et Cie?

Desperate, the board at last turned to Washington for advice. His reply was cold:

"In the present instance, as I neither know the extent of the object in view, nor the means to be employed to effect them, it is not in my power to pass any judgment upon the subject."

Washington was having his own troubles. It was hard to train soldiers who were only half dressed and were weak from hunger. A man whose toes have been frostbitten does not drill well. It would not take much to bring about an explosion at Valley Forge. The officers, everybody, feared that this might happen.

Conceivably Congress did not trust even the officers, for on February 3 it decreed that every officer in the Army should subscribe to the following oath:

"I, ______ ______, do acknowledge the United States of America to be free, independent and sovereign states, and declare that the people thereof owe no allegiance or obedience to George the Third, King of Great Britain; and I do renounce, refuse and abjure any allegiance or obedience to him; and I do swear (or affirm) that I will to the utmost of my power support, maintain and defend the said United States against the said King George the Third, and his heirs, and successors, and his and their abettors, assistants and adherents, and will serve the United States in the office of ______, which I now hold, with fidelity, according to the best of my skill and understanding. So help me God."

What this was expected to produce, aside from a sense of outrage in the men who signed it and a suspicion on the part of the world that all was not well at Valley Forge, is not on record; yet neither is there a record of any officer, whatever he may have thought of the thing, refusing to sign.

There was no abatement of the cold; and the wind from the northeast was icy, relentless. After the Christmas storm and an even heavier fall late in January, there was very little snow; but there was a great deal of cruelly cold rain, which sometimes turned to sleet. Nor were there any longer trees to give at least a partial, temporary protection.

The threat of mutiny grew . . . and grew . . . If it happened it would be by spontaneous combustion. No telltale wisp of smoke would first be seen—or smelled. No subversive influence was at work here; whispers were not passed about; there was no plot, for the men weren't organized on their own. Nevertheless, each day the thing got nearer.

The soldiers were acting in a strange manner. They were not openly defiant, but they were shifty of eye and they muttered among themselves. It got so that many of the officers were afraid to enter the huts, just as British navy officers feared for their lives if obliged to go down into the forecastle. It was best not to turn one's back upon such men.

Sometimes when an officer passed along a brigade street, doors would be opened behind him, and men would chant "No meat, no soldier!" after which, as he spun around, the doors would be slammed.

One night, for all the world like prisoners in a great penitentiary, starting at no signal, the men began to pound on the walls of their huts, making catcalls and bird caws, calling out, again and again, in unison, *"We—want—meat!"* The officers did not interfere, though they stood by, in a sweat of nervousness; and after a while the demonstration died.

Until a little while ago they had made many jokes about their pitiful condition. "How are you, soldier?" "All wet, thank 'e, and I hope you are the same." At a rumor that blue and buff was being debated as the official Continental colors: "Well, we've got the buff all right." There was a song popular among the redcoats, since it made fun of the natives, and as they had done in the case of "Yankee Doodle" the Continental soldiers took it up as their own:

"First we'll take a pinch of snuff,
And then a drink of water,
And then we'll say, How do you do?
And that's a Yankee supper."

They no longer sang this at Valley Forge. They sang nothing. Silent men are dangerous men. These did not even croak, or caw. But they could quit. Would they?

Chapter Twenty-one

THE COMMANDER in Chief's mail, coming and going, was tremendous. He could handle it. Like Caesar, he would wear out a platoon of secretaries—and then take up the pen himself. He did not like paper work, and did not pride himself on his ability as a writer. There are no flourishes in his letters.

He wrote to Israel (Old Put) Putnam, major general in command of the Hudson Highlands, that his army was "literally in a starving condition," and directed him to cease diverting cattle on the hoof for the use of his own men.

That same day, February 6, he wrote to another staunch Connecticut Yankee, the governor, Jonathan Trumbull, that "The present situation of the Army is the most Melancholy that can be conceived," and urged him to send whatever supplies he could. One might rely on "Brother Jonathan," he used to say, thus perhaps being the first to give a name to what was to be for many years ("Uncle Sam" did not come into existence until the War of 1812) the classic American political figure. The following day he wrote much the same letter to Henry Champion, deputy commissary general of purchases for the eastern department, and a copy of this was sent to Peter Colt, the commissary general, who appears to have been a figurehead. Governor Trumbull and Colonel Champion went to work at once, and soon caravans of cattle were trudging their way toward Valley Forge. Connecticut had always been a good provider, both for its own and for the Continental troops.

The Commander in Chief kept up a running correspondence with red-faced, peppery little William Smallwood, the brigadier in command of the camp near Wilmington, Delaware, pushing him on to greater foraging efforts in Delaware and Maryland.

He wrote to Congress: "I can declare that, no Man, in my opinion, ever had his measures more impeded than I have, by every department of the Army. Since the Month of July, we have had no assistance from the Quarter Master Genl. and to want of assistance from this department the Commissary Genl. charges great part of his deficiency."

He wrote to Lafayette, gently, quietly, to dissuade him from a rash attempt upon New York City, and to assure him that he would not be abased in the eyes of the world, and that his honor was as bright and his reputation as high as ever.

His correspondence with Sir William Howe, whom he was never to meet, was sporadic and sometimes acrimonious, though always, of course, formally polite. It concerned an exchange of prisoners. Washington—it is hard to see why, since the man was after his job—was straining every nerve, all that winter, to arrange for a return of his second-in-command, Charles Lee. But occasionally he would write to Howe about something else. Earlier, Howe's pet dog, like so many of the men, had become lost in the fog that swathed the battle of Germantown, and, complete with collar and identifying tag, strayed as far as Pennypacker's Mill before it was picked up and taken to headquarters. Washington promptly arranged for its return, together with a pleasant note, under a flag of truce. "Everyone is captivated by this general," wrote a Hessian.[76]

Not quite everybody. Patrick Henry, governor of Virginia, sent to the Commander in Chief an anonymous letter he had received. It deplored Washington's "mob," and declared that "A Gates, a Lee, or a Conway would in a few weeks render them an irresistible body of men." Washington wrote back, March 28, when returning the letter, that he believed the handwriting to be that of a physician who "has been elaborate, and studied in his professions of regard for me," namely, Dr. Benjamin Rush of Philadelphia.[77] He confessed that he was not astounded: "My caution to avoid any thing, that could injure the service, prevented me from communicating, but to very few of my friends, the intrigues of a faction, which I know was formed against me, since it might serve to publish our internal dissentions; but their own restless Zeal to advance their views has too clearly betrayed them, and made concealment, on my part, fruitless. I cannot precisely mark the extent of their views, but it appeared in general, that General Gates was to be exalted, on the ruin of my reputation and influence. This I am authorized to say, from undeniable facts in my own possession, from publications, the evident scope of which, could not be mistaken, and from private detractions industriously circulated. General Mifflin, it is commonly supposed, bore the second part in the Cabal; and General Conway, I know was a very Active and malignant Partisan . . ."[78]

This much is in the handwriting of a secretary, Robert Hanson Harrison, but Washington has added in his own hand: "but I have good reasons to believe, that their machinations have recoiled most sensibly upon themselves."

He received from Richard Henry Lee, who was back in Virginia, the report of a scandalous pamphlet printed in England and reprinted in New York, supposedly written by a prisoner, no less a personage than Washington's own Negro valet, Billy Lee (who had never been captured and was in camp right then, and who couldn't write anyway). "The design of the forger is evident," Lee wrote, "and no doubt it gained him a good beefsteak from his masters. I would send you this pamphlet, if it were not too bulky for the post, as it might serve to amuse your leisure hours during the inaction of winter."

Lee, in Williamburg, had an odd idea of what life was like at Valley Forge. There were no "leisure hours" for the Commander in Chief at this time. He didn't know the meaning of "inaction."

On February 14 he wrote to Governor William Livingston of New Jersey: "This is the second time, in the course of the present year, that we have been on the point of dissolution, and I know not whether the melancholy event may not take place."

He was forever writing to governors, as to Congressmen, and to personal friends.

On February 16, to Governor George Clinton of New York: "For some days past, there has been little less than a famine in camp. A part of the army has been a week without any kind of flesh, and the rest three or four days. Naked and starving as they are, we cannot help admiring the imcomparable patience and fidelity of the soldiery, that they have not been ere this excited by their sufferings, to a general mutiny and dispersion."

On February 18, desperate, he dictated to Alexander Hamilton an address to the people of New Jersey, Pennsylvania, Maryland, and Virginia, appealing for aid; and he sent this to the four governors with a personal note to each asking that the address be posted and published as soon and as widely as possible.

He got a letter from the Rev. William Gordon, asking anxiously if it was true that he might resign. He replied, in his own hand: "I have said, and I still do say, that there is not an Officer in the Service of the United States that would return to the sweets of domestic life with more heart felt joy than I should; but I would have this declaration, accompanied by these Sentiments, that while the public are satisfied with my endeavours I mean not to shrink in the cause; but, the moment her voice, not that of faction, calls upon me to resign, I shall do it with as much pleasure as ever the weary traveller retired to rest."

The gentleman always, he added a P.S. "Mrs. Washington who is now with me joins in best respects to Mrs. Gordon."

Henry Laurens, president of the Continental Congress, one winter morning as he was about to enter the little court house in Center Square, York, was handed a letter which somebody —he never did identify the man—said he had just picked up from the steps. Laurens glanced at it, and thrust it into a pocket. He made no mention of it to Congress that day, as clearly he had been meant to do, and afterward he sent the thing to General Washington.

It was called "Thoughts of a Freeman," and contained forty-five statements, many of which severely critized Washington's judgment as commander in chief, also his too-high seat: "I believe . . . that the people of America have been guilty of idolatry, by making a man their god; and the God of heaven and earth will convince them by woeful experience, that he is only a man; that no good may be expected from the standing army, until Baal and his worshippers are banished from the camp."

There was nothing new in this paper, but it was well assembled, a neatly organized document. Laurens wrote that his impulse, after glancing at it, had been to throw the thing into the fire; but on second thought he had sent it to the Commander in Chief as a matter of morbid interest. Washington returned it, thanking Laurens and asking him to read the paper before Congress—something Laurens never did do.

"My Enemies take an ungenerous advantage of me," Washington wrote. "They know I cannot combat their insinuations, however injurious, without disclosing secrets, it is of the utmost moment to conceal. But why should I expect to be exempt from censure; the unfailing lot of an elevated station?"

So he went on working.

Chapter Twenty-two

No muskets were fired, no cannons boomed, yet a powerful section of Congress was waging war against the Continental army. The ranks of those who feared a standing force were greater even than those who thought that George Washington was not the man to lead it.

Washington himself intensified this opposition by his stand against the militia system. It was a stand banked by logic. Too many times at a critical hour the militia of this state or of that—they were equally guilty—had failed him. Militiamen came to camp erratically, so that their presence could not be counted upon; and they usually came in the summer—hence the expression "summer soldier" for one who will help only at his own convenience, going away when bad weather sets in. They were at least as well equipped as the regulars, and often their equipment was better; but their officers, who had been chosen on the ground of personal popularity, could be sluggards or fools or both, knowing little of the military facts of life, being rather village-green paraders, brave under a cockade, less admirable in a trench. A militiaman would serve for two or three or even four months, and then, just as he was beginning to understand things, to take his place, to earn his rations, he'd leave. The over-all strategic situation did not mean anything to him. Hundreds quit the army on the eve of the battle of Long Island, hundreds more just before the battle of Princeton; and Washington, time after time in the course of the retreat through New Jersey, had been obliged to give up defensible positions just because some militia company that should have been there had simply disappeared, as though by evaporation, never to be seen again.

Congress, by a resolve of July 29, 1775, had decided to pay the private six and two-thirds dollars a month. Thus in the very beginning the U. S. soldier became—as he has continued to be—the highest paid in the world.

That statement needs qualification. Many if not most of the European soldiers, the rank and file, either were unaspiring peasants who had barely been able to grind out a miserable existence, or convicted felons given their choice between the musket and the noose: in either case they were lucky to be alive. The typical American private, if there could be said to be such a person, was not like that. He had not lived in luxury, but he might well be the son of a small landowner or merchant, and have a solid background—and hopes of an inheritance. Six and two-thirds dollars a month, on a meager diet, did not dazzle such lads.

Moreover, the pay was in Continental money, which from the start had been weak and at the time of the Valley Forge winter was plunging. And all prices, everywhere, had gone up.

In accord with the "leveling" idea, there was little differance between the pay of officers and that of the men. This encouraged fraternization, a practice approved by some New Englanders but frowned upon as bad for discipline by virtually all Southern and Middle-State leaders.

The rate of pay was especially hard on the lower ranking

officers. Congress, when prodded, with no very good grace raised their pay by one-third; but even after this had been done, a captain, say, in the Continental army was getting only about half of what a British captain got, and the latter, unless he belonged to a swank regiment, was offered the chance to live much more cheaply. Also, the Britisher's commission was a piece of property that had a fixed value and could be sold, or even, in certain circumstances, pawned.

"They [the officers] are not vastly riveted to the honor of starving their families for the sake of being in the army," Henry Knox wrote to John Adams, a leader of the no-standing-army group. "I am not speaking for myself, but I am speaking in the behalf of a great number of worthy men who wish to do the country every service in their power at a less price than the ruin of themselves and families."[79]

On June 26, 1776, Congress grudgingly granted a ten-dollar bounty for each enlistment. This was pale, as the Commander in Chief had warned. Why should a man enlist for three years for ten dollars when he could join a militia for six months or even less and get twenty, twenty-five, or thirty? For the states in this respect had very early started to compete against one another and against the federal government.

A few months later Congress, Washington egging it, granted a land bounty as well, ranging from five hundred acres for each general or colonel to one hundred acres for a private, at the same time doubling the cash bounty. It also guaranteed each recruit one suit of clothes a year—or twenty dollars cash if the man supplied his own—a suit of clothes being defined as two pairs of hose, two pairs of shoes, a hat or leather cap, two pairs of overalls, two shirts, one pair of breeches, and a leather or woolen waistcoat with sleeves.

The discontent remained. Patriotism, as Washington had pointed out, can go just so far.

Throughout that winter of 1777–78, the Commander in Chief, with all the other things he had to do, was engaged at long distance—Valley Forge to York is about eighty miles—in trying to get from Congress an agreement to provide half-pay for officers and men alike, in addition to land grants. Congress, and particularly the Adams bloc, balked. They saw the proposal as a move toward militarism. There were those who became almost apoplectic when half-pay was mentioned, and they were in high places.

Washington had his finger in the hole in the dike. He refused Sullivan a furlough; he talked that redoubtable fisherman John Glover out of resigning; but the junior officers were another matter. Already the war had lasted much longer than anybody had expected, and the end was by no means in sight. They had to think of the folks at home. Not only was the present grim, but the future, unless headquarters won its tussle with the Congress, was utterly black. No man could make a career out of a temporary shift. Many junior officers resigned; others, who wouldn't risk an open show, got furloughs from which they never came back.

The North Carolina legislature came up with a resolution which, if it had been copied by other states, would greatly have helped to keep the Continental army together. It resolved that any North Carolina officers who resigned from the federal army without a good reason, a reason certified by the Commander in Chief, could no longer qualify to hold any civil or military post within the gift of the state. That was the kind of co-operation the states too seldom gave, and Washington approved it, thanking North Carolina. But this law had come too late.

Washington fought hard with what he had. On April 2, Congress voted unanimously to postpone action, a set-back; but at last, on May 15, it consented to a compromise—half-pay for officers for seven years after the end of the war, with the proviso that no such officer would get his half-pay if he was in the service of the federal government or that of any state, and for privates and non-coms a flat eighty-dollar cash bonus, this being equal to about one year's pay for a private.

The vote was twenty-three to two, both dissenters being from New England: James Lovell of Massachusetts, the same disagreeable man who had berated Lafayette in such bad French, afterward slamming the door in his face; and Oliver Wolcott of Connecticut.

This was a victory without fanfare, a victory not often noted in the history books but of incalculable importance to the problem at hand—that of somehow holding the army together. It was not as good as the Commander in Chief had hoped for, but was as good as he could get; and it did help to bolster his wobbling prestige.

Chapter Twenty-three

THE HORSE is a noble animal, but an animal that the American colonists by and large took for granted. Almost everybody moved on horseback, since, except in or near cities where the roads might be passable, coaches could not be managed for most of the year, while oxcarts were too slow.

The thickly wooded wilderness was not suited to the horse, a friend the Indian of those parts had never known. Virginia and Maryland, where a cavalier class had settled, were exceptions. In those colonies there were races as early as the seventeenth century; though clearly the race horses themselves were not held in high esteem, for there is no record of any of them or of their breeding. The first thoroughbred to be brought to an American colony—Virginia, in 1730—was Bulle Rock, by Darley Arabian out of a mare by the Byerly Turk. By that time racing had spread, if in hesitant fashion, to the Carolinas in the south, New Jersey and New York in the north; but it was not organized racing, and it did not draw large crowds or leave telling records. By and large, up and down the colonies, the horse was looked upon as a working animal.

Even as such it was not rated the best. In many places, and especially in New England, the ox was thought a better beast.

An ox could work all day pulling a plow across a steep hillside —without going lame as a horse would. If it was slower it was stronger, more durable. It didn't need shoes. It cost about the same in the first place, ate about the same, required less care, and lived longer.

One of the first orders issued from headquarters after Valley Forge had been occupied, prohibited private saddle horses in camp except by special permission. There is no way of knowing how much this was disobeyed.

Saddle horses were to be alloted fourteen pounds of hay and six quarts of oats a day, draft horses a little more depending upon the type of work they did; but it is to be doubted that many of them got that. It has been estimated that fifteen hundred horses died of starvation that winter at Valley Forge. No monument has been erected to them.

Exposure might have had much to do with those deaths. The field officers almost to a man, plus their aides and orderlies, lived in farmhouses several miles from camp, traveling back and forth of course on horseback, but no doubt nighting their mounts in the farmers' stables. In the camp itself all timber had been used for huts, fires, breastworks, and the abatis, not to mention the bridge, twelve feet wide, that Sullivan's men were building across the Schuylkill; if there were any stables at all in camp they were inadequate. Men who had no other kind of bedding surely appropriated a great deal of the hay and straw meant for horses. Even in the surrounding countryside, notably opened to the north by the new bridge, equine quarters were not extensive. When in the spring the commissary general of prisoners, Elias Boudinot, visited Valley Forge, the nearest farm with accommodations for his horses was *eighteen miles* away.

Was the horse thought of as "unclean"? The prospects of eating the flesh of any animal that has lingeringly expired is not a lifter of the heart; yet an empty stomach can endure a great deal. There are records of those poor beasts being buried—or rather *not* being buried soon enough—but there is no record that one or any part of one was consumed as

Commander in chief and Staff. *Courtesy New York Public Library; Picture Collection*

food. Dogs were not spared on the terrible march through Maine at the time of the first "iruption into Canada" under Benedict Arnold in 1775, but the horses at Valley Forge were put underneath the soil.

George Washington was an enthusiastic fox hunter and one of the best horsemen in the land. His white Nelson was as familiar a sight at Valley Forge, and as much admired, as Anthony Wayne's gray Nancy.

Washington has been scolded for failing to use his cavalry properly, so as to shorten the war.[80] This is hindsight. When Washington took over the command it was the command of a siege, where horses were of use only to carry couriers and to move cannon. Once the siege was successful he was concerned with countering Howe's next pounce, which he guessed to be—as it turned out to be—upon New York. At that time he had but scattered, uncertain small bodies of horsemen, even those being in the nature of dragoons—that is, mounted infantry. By far the largest and most impressive of these groups came from Connecticut, some four hundred young men, all volunteers, who were supplying their own mounts and equipment. Members of this corps, a frilly one, had put it as a condition of their service that because they took care of their own horses they must be exempt from ordinary army chores, such as standing guard. Washington, who was having a hard time enforcing even the most rudimentary discipline anyway, thought that such an exemption would smell of favoritism and be bad for morale; so he said no. Whereupon the Connecticut men went home. This was done at a time when Howe was about to land in overwhelming force and Washington needed every soldier he could get. It could not have given him a good opinion of what might be called the cavalry temperament.

In the retreat across New Jersey the Continental army could surely have used mounted troops to good advantage, again and again. So, for that matter, could the British army, which likewise was poorly provided with saddle horses. If it had been possible to predict that the war would converge on the central states and the eastern seaboard, no doubt other arrangements would have been made. But it was at first thought that the principal battleground might be in Maine, northern Vermont, northern New York, or Canada—hilly, densely forested terrain where cavalry would have been a drag. Later, after Washington had retreated across the Delaware, a goodly segment of the generals thought that the war might degenerate into guerilla fighting in western Pennsylvania, a place of mountains where, again, cavalry would have been in the way.

In later years, when the war had moved south and conditions for horse maneuver were ideal, Washington showed a quick appreciation of the value of cavalry, and applied it.

His attitude at Valley Forge is best summed up by himself, in his long, considered report to the Committe of Congress with the Army (the Committee of Conference), dated January 29, 1778. The part of that report that pertains to cavalry is actually in the handwriting of Alexander Hamilton, but there can be no doubt that Washington went over every word of it with the greatest care—as indeed he did of the whole report—and in a few places he has added some words of his own.

"The benefits arising from a superiority in horse, are obvious to those who have experienced them. Independent of such as you may derive of it in the field of action, it enables you, very materially, to controul the inferior and subordinate motions of an enemy, and to impede their knowledge of what you are doing, while it gives you every advantage of superior intelligence and, consequently, both facilitates your enterprizes against them and obstructs theirs against you. In a defensive war as in our case it is peculiarly desirable; because it affords great protection to the country, and is a barrier to those inroads and depradations upon the inhabitants, which are inevitable when the superiority lies on the side of the invaders. The enemy fully sensible of the advantages, are taking all the pains in their power, to acquire an ascendency in this respect, to defeat which I would propose an augmentation of our cavalry."

What your cavalryman desires above all is dash; and there was precious little of it at Valley Forge. The head of that branch, Count Casimir Pulaski, whose Polish estates had been stripped by the Russians, had fire enough for a dozen. That observant Yankee, Albigence Waldo, saw him as a man of "hardly middling Stature. . . . sharp countenance and lively air." However, Pulaski was incorrigibly the foreigner. He never did comprehend American ways, nor did he learn enough English to make himself understood. He didn't get along with his subordinates, and might have suspected his superiors. He was romance incarnate, and probably not unaware of this fact. Later in the war he was to die gloriously, charging at the head of his men in the best cavalry tradition; but it can hardly be thought that during the winter of 1777–78 he was happy.

A brigadier, he was seldom in camp, though he reported directly to the Commander in Chief. His base, most of the time, was Trenton, New Jersey, and his work, most of the time —and he hated it—was foraging.

Under Pulaski were the First Continental Regiment of Light Dragoons, always called Bland's Virginia horse; Sheldon's Connecticut regiment; Baylor's regiment, the Third, made up largely of men from Virginia and Maryland; and Moylan's Fourth regiment, made up of men from Maryland and Pennsylvania.[81]

Among the colonels, Stephen Moylan glittered the brightest. He was that same "accomplished Irish gentleman resident among us . . . of habits and manners not exactly suited to the difficulties of the times," who had been unable to make a go of the quartermaster-generalship, causing it to be given back to Mifflin. He succeeded to the command of the brigade after Pulaski, in March, resigned to start his own "Cavalry Legion" made up of foreigners, in part mounted, in part on foot.

The Continental cavalry had brilliant uniforms—on paper. These included jack boots, though in truth in the winter of 1777–78 the rider who had as much as a pair of shoes was a rarity. They included, too, a brass helmet, striped with leopard skin from stem to stern, which, alas, was to remain a designer's fond dream. Moylan, never forgetful of his birth—he was the first president of the Friendly Sons of St. Patrick—and believing that a special arm of the service like the cavalry should have its distinctive uniform, campaigned for a bright green coat. His men eventually were issued this coat—years later, just before they were disbanded. At and around Valley Forge, like the others, they wore anything they could get. Many were garbed in coats seized after the victory at Saratoga, the red coats so long a characteristic, though nobody knows why,[82] of the British army; this was to cause a great deal of confusion.

At that time and in that place there was a cavalry captain who outshone them all, though the glory of his exploits has faded. Alan McLane was a rich young Delawarean, unpredictable, irregular; and his escapes and escapades—for some of them could hardly be called more than that—were of the stuff that folk operas are made. It would appear that he was captured, or almost captured, every day. He was not one for large forces, and never went out with more than a handful of men, often indeed being alone. He did not scorn to wear a disguise, something the very thought of which would have horrified most officers of any army. His deeds of derring-do were told around every fire, and whenever he came to camp his trim, slim figure, astride the high-stepping stallion Saladin, was cheered.

It is noteworthy that while Virginia was first among the thirteen states in the matter of cavalry, both as to men and mounts, Connecticut was an unexpected and very good second, having more than all the other eleven put together. Connecticut was the only New England state to contribute any cavalry at all to the Continental army.

The oldest organized cavalry outfit in the country, the perky, exclusive Philadelphia Light Horse, served at Valley Forge. It was a small group, yet it was to see a lot of action.

At about this time Captain Bartholomew von Heer formed the Marechause Light Dragoons, made up mostly of Germans like himself; and in May this company, taking over from various militia groups, who had always quarreled about precedent, became headquarters guard and provost guard.

Chapter Twenty-four

WOULD THAT winter never end? Would the wind from the northeast never cease to blow? Shivering, sick, red-eyed from smoke, the soldiers clinging to that stump-studded hillside clung to only one other thing—their faith in the General. If in that season there had been any rumor that George Washington was dead, or even that he was ill, it might have started a panic.

He had inured himself to public acclaim, and could incline his head graciously, if not far, on the proper occasion. There is no reason to believe that he enjoyed this; but he did have an inkling of how much he meant to the men.

No thought of sport could have come to this outdoor man at Valley Forge. The countryside was suitable for it, especially now that his soldiers had burned all the rail fences, but he would not even have dreamed of doing what Wellington on the Peninsula a little later was to do—send home for his hounds. But as often as he could get away from that mountain of paper work at Deborah Hewes's house, he would ride around the camp, conscientiously exhibiting himself.

This must have been harder to do now that Martha had come. She arrived February 10, a plump, somewhat dumpy woman with a quick smile. Everybody liked her, everybody called her "my lady," and there was vast amusement when, as occasionally happened, she referred to General Washington as "the old man." To a person brought up as she had been in a huge house, there was little routine work at Valley Forge, and she busied herself making soups and jellies for those in hospital, visiting them every day. She was the richest woman in America, not bright, but very good-natured.

Martha knew the truth about her husband's health. Few others in camp did.

His appearance and past alike, his manner as well, brought about the belief that he was indestructible, or virtually so, in physique a superman. Planter, hunter, hard rider, as a youth a champion wrestler, he stood six feet four and a half inches tall, and because of his erect carriage showed even taller than that. He had spent many months on the wild frontier, surveying, fighting Indians. His complexion, though sallow and pitted by smallpox, was weatherbeaten. His courage in battle was phenomenal, a freak: he didn't seem to know the meaning of fear.

Yet the man had suffered more than his share of ailments, and had spent a good part of his life in bed. It can be assumed —there is no record—that he had had the usual children's diseases. Malaria came early, when he was in his teens, and it recurred again and again through the rest of his life. He had that smallpox, a severe case, at nineteen, and a long spell of acute pleurisy after his return from the Barbados when he was barely twenty. In Braddock's campaign of 1755 he was laid up for a long while with what appears to have been influenza, and on the day of the battle of the Monongahela had barely been able to mount, to sit in saddle; yet though he had two horses killed under him that day, while his uniform was pierced by bullets in four places, he still was able to command the retreat, saving what was left of the army. Later still, but before his marriage, he was to suffer dysentery, a very severe attack, and something that might have been typhoid. Many times he had been expected, and himself expected, to die.

Though his mother was a durable old body, the other side of the family could hardly be called long-lived. His paternal grandfather had died at thirty-seven, his father at forty-nine, his half-brother at thirty-three.

The Commander in Chief himself, however, at Valley Forge never reported to sick bay, and if a physician ever was summoned to Deborah Hewes's house that visit was kept quiet. He just couldn't afford to be ill. There was no time—and there was too much at stake.[83]

His posterity has been accused of elevating George Washington to a pedestal. This is silly. He was always up there. He assumed that position naturally and of his own accord, for the reason that he believed it his duty to do so. It is inconceivable that he should ever be anywhere else *but* on a pedestal. All at-

George Washington's Headquarters at Valley Forge. *Courtesy Valley Forge State Park Commission*

tempts to "humanize" him, pointing up his temper, his stubbornness, his sensitivity, his lack of imagination, are vulgar and inept. He was not human. He was a god. The men at Valley Forge knew that. It is even possible that George Washington himself knew it.

Martha from the beginning had showed her determination to share as much of her husband's hardships as she could, coming to him at each camp. Washington's financial arrangement with Congress was simple: he would serve without salary but expected to have his expenses paid. Martha, so long as she was in camp, quite properly was written off as an expense.

By any standards their establishment was a humble one. By their own it must have been downright squalor. Washington habitually had five field officers at each dinner, a meal then held early in the afternoon: the major general of the day, the brigadier of the day, two lieutenant colonels, and a brigade major. These, together with his aides, nine in number, made a total of fifteen at the table including the General himself, if there weren't any guests. Martha fitted easily into this company, being used to men. If the talk was of war, as it usually was, she just ignored it.

The dinner of February 22, a day not yet declared a national holiday, should have been a gala one at Deborah Hewes's house. For several reasons it was not. In the first place, there was a curious *doubleness* about it, since his own state of Virginia had not, as Pennsylvania had, adopted the new time, the Gregorian calendar: in Virginia, by the old calendar, the Julian, he had been forty-six years old for eleven days now. Besides, birthday anniversaries can be depressing; and the General was not feeling remarkably well. He retired immediately after dinner, knowing that he needed rest; and when a little later some Pennsylvania bandsmen, a fife and drum corps, came down the hill to serenade him, he listened but did not go out. Martha did go out, afterward, and she thanked them in the name of the General, and, likewise in his name, passed out fifteen shillings as a tip. Washington of course put this on his expense account.

Unworried, then—for ordinary illness could never touch a man like that—the musicians trudged back to their huts. The wind was rising. It would be a cold night.

Chapter Twenty-five

ON THE FIRST day of December, 1777, there stepped ashore at Portsmouth, New Hampshire, a thick-set man of middle height, heavy-featured with light brown hair, brown-gray eyes, and an easy intelligent smile. He wore a red-and-blue uniform of his own design, and around his neck hung a medal almost the size of a soup plate—the star of the Order of Fidelity of Baden-Durlach.

He was forty-eight. His legs were much too short for his great

Major General Baron von Steuben. *Courtesy New York Public Library Picture Collection*

torso, and when he walked it was with a waddle; but on horseback he cut a magnificent figure, verily a giant.

This was Friedrich Wilhelm Ludolf Gerhard Augustin, Baron von Steuben. He talked lightly—in French or in German, for he could not speak a word of English—of his lieutenant-generalship in some unspecified European army, his estate in Swabia, his close association with Frederick the Great, who, he intimated, must be missing him.

In his suite, besides his secretary, Duponceau, and his aide, De Pontiere (he was to be joined, a few days later in Boston, by another aide, L'Enfant, the future layer-out of Washington, D.C.), were his valet, Carl Vogel, and his chef, De Romani. At his heels trotted his Italian greyhound, Azor.

This personage sat down and penned an offer of his services to the Continental cause, and this, together with his letters of introduction, he sent off to General Washington, who was then in the camp at Whitemarsh, Pennsylvania.

He did not wait long, for Washington was punctilious about his correspondence. The answer, though hardly gushing, was polite. It congratulated Baron von Steuben on his safe arrival; it acknowledged receipt of the credentials; and it invited him to present himself at headquarters whenever this was convenient.

Steuben took his time. It was February 23 before he arrived in the Continental camp, by that time at Valley Forge.

One of his biographers, noting with joy that Steuben was "a systematic, circumstantial and deliberate liar,"[84] suggests that he was a creature of that bright and lively thing, Benjamin Franklin's imagination.

It is conceivable. Franklin, with his pawky humor, his spectacles, his coonskin cap, had recently taken Paris by storm; but this had not gone to his head. He had met Steuben and realized at once that here was the very man the Continental army needed. But Franklin knew the situation in Congress, from which he had just come. Any further foreign adventurers would be examined with a devastating thoroughness. They might even be turned down on sight, without being given a chance to open their mouths, as had happened to the Marquis de Lafayette. Something else was needed, something extra, to impress the Congressmen, also the generals. Franklin might then and there have devised the appurtenances and coached Steuben in the part. It is possible. The pieces fit. But there is no proof.[85]

For the man who had been born Wilhelm Steube was no baron. He had picked up the *n* and the title, along with the other names and also the *von*—or, as he himself preferred it, *de*—somewhere along the line. He had no estate in Swabia or anywhere else. He never did spell out that nation in which he was said to have been a lieutenant general,[86] and before he came to these shores there is no record of his having held any higher military rank than that of major. If he ever saw Frederick the Great it was from a distance.

But he was a good soldier. He knew what to expect, and he turned on all his charm.

The Congressmen and the members of the Board of War were delighted, and even Washington, though he was cautious, nodded approval.

The idea of an inspector-generalship of the Continental army was by no means new. Baron d'Erendt had first proposed it, and at the end of October Washington had put the plan before a council made up of five major generals, including Lafayette, and ten brigadiers, including Conway. The council was unanimously in favor of it, but the plan never was adopted by Congress. It had called for an inspector general who was to be directly under the commander in chief. When a little later Thomas Conway achieved his promotion, he advanced his own plan, which called for an inspector general independent of the commander in chief and answerable only to the Board of War. It was this plan that was adopted, and Conway was appointed to the office. He never really served, since he could accomplish nothing without the co-operation of Washington, and now he was far away—with the army of the north.

Steuben instantly was looked upon as a possible candidate for this office, if Conway could be pushed out. Perhaps he even proposed himself. But if he did, he added the suggestion that the Board of War wait and see how he worked out, how he fitted, before they assigned him to any rank.

This modesty, so unexpected, so thoroughly un-European, left them agasp. But Steuben went further. With engaging candor he announced that he had no money, and this was why he would be obliged to ask for his expenses, though of course he would serve without pay. The expenses? He had given up sundry "places and posts of honor in Germany" worth about six hundred guineas a year. He never did say what those "places and posts" were.

The Board of War agreed informally to six hundred guineas a year. It appointed him *acting* inspector general with rank to be determined later. Gravely he thanked the members. He was assigned to quarters and went right to bed.

He was up before dawn and, while Carl Vogel combed and clubbed his hair, he drank a cup of chocolate and smoked his morning pipe. The sun was rising and drums were beating the reveille when he got on his horse and rode to the parade ground for his first day's work.

Chapter Twenty-six

He has been called the only popular drillmaster. He didn't pose; he was no equestrian statue barking orders. He got right down off his horse and showed how to handle a musket by handling one himself, a demonstration that even in the "leveled" army of the United States was without precedent, causing men to leap. For there were men watching. There always were men watching when Steuben conducted his drills. Not only was it fascinating to see an associate of Frederick the Great, dismounted, handling an ordinary musket like an ordinary trooper

—only much better than the average trooper could have done—but the newcomer's vocabulary excited interest everywhere in camp. He could swear, and did, in French and German; and the first word of English he picked up was "goddam." Progress, linguistically, thereafter was slower; but he never forgot that first word. He had assigned to him an aide, a young captain from New York named Ben Walker, who was fluent in French, and when Steuben, red of face, after windmilling his arms and stamping in rage and shouting, would run out of words the men could understand, he'd turn to Walker, spreading his hands.

"Tiens, mon ami, mon bon ami! Goddam de gaucheries of dese badants! Je ne puis plus! *You* curse dem, Valker!"

This was always a great moment, and Steuben played up to it. Nor was this wholly a matter of vanity, of which the man admittedly did have his share. Anybody could see that the more troopers who turned out to watch the daily drill, the sooner all would learn what was required.

And a great deal was required. If Steuben had been appointed to break in a raw army, men who had never before spent a day in camp, his task would not have been so hard. What he got was an army of soldiers who thought they knew something—and had it all wrong.

He was appalled by the conditions he found. Not only were the costumes these men wore anything but uniform (he had been prepared for that), not only were the muskets of all sorts and sizes (this condition gradually was growing better, as arms came from France), but seemingly no attempt had been made to set any manner of standard. The number of officers in proportion to privates differed in different parts of the camp; and the officers weren't there half the time anyway. A regiment might be composed of three or four platoons, or five, or nine: the lone Canadian regiment had twenty-two. The last person to ask about this was the colonel. There were regiments of more than six hundred men, regiments of fewer than sixty. A company might be of almost any size. So it was too with squads—where squads had been designated.

It might have been thought that Steuben would have imposed either the French or the Prussian manual of arms and system of drill upon his new charges, or even the British system—for which, however, he had scant respect. He didn't. He made up one of his own to fit the conditions he found. Simplicity was its keynote.

One of the things that shocked him most about conditions at camp was the casual attitude of the officers, many or even most of whom had aped the British attitude toward drill—that it was a tedious chore and fit only for sergeants and such, not for gentlemen. In Steuben's army—and he made this clear the very first day—the officers must drill the men directly, not through non-coms. There was some grumbling at this, but Washington backed him and he won his way.

Like other observers he expressed astonishment at the ability of the men to live under such conditions. Their independence, their individuality, amused but didn't disconcert him; and he adapted himself to it, seeing at once that these were not the stupid cowed peasants or sullen jailbirds he had been used to in Europe.

"The genius of this nation is not in the least to be compared with that of the Prussians, Austrians or French," he wrote to an old comrade in arms, Baron von Gaudy. "You say to your soldier 'Do this' and he doeth it; but I am obliged to say 'This is the reason why you ought to do that'; and then he does it."[87]

He was his own best example. If he drove the men, he drove himself even harder. In young Laurens' phrase, he worked "with the zeal of a lieutenant anxious for promotion."

And the men responded. They might have been expected to rebel, weak and battered as they were, and neglected. "We have lately been in a most alarming situation for want of provisions," Laurens had written his father less than a week before the arrival of Steuben. "The soldiers were scarcely restrained from mutiny by the eloquence and management of our officers."[88] Men in such a mood might be expected to rebel when a foreigner who couldn't even speak English was put over them and insisted upon hours of grind, of work, far from the fires. They didn't. They loved it.

"Why should we do what he says, when he's nothing but another Hessian?" growled some, to whom every German was a Hessian, and hateful. But this soon passed.

Oddly, one of Steuben's first reforms, and one he pushed most vigorously, was opposed by officers and men alike. This was a cutting-down of the number of servants in camp. He stood aghast when he saw that virtually every officer, even the ensigns, had at least one batman, some having two or three or four. Other privates, while not working regularly for one officer, hired themselves out to do odd jobs, personal jobs, for various superiors, whether for pitifully little pay or for no pay at all, but simply the privilege of getting out of guard duty. Half the camp, it sometimes seemed, was waiting on the other half.

Efficiency, not democracy, was what Wilhelm Steuben was interested in. How could he train men who were forever being excused from drill in order to polish the boots of some major who thought he needed more attendants than a field marshal abroad? Steuben was honestly scandalized. He stormed. In the end, and at the expense of much hard feeling, he more or less got his way, though he never was able to eradicate the evil, the Continental army remaining ludicrously over-servanted.

"The soldiers were scattered about in every direction," he wrote in a private memorandum at this time. "The army was looked upon as a nursery for servants, and every one deemed it his right to have a valet; several thousand soldiers were employed in this way. . . . With regard to their military discipline, I may safely say no such thing existed."[89]

This even engulfed his own military household. Steuben's native love of pomp assuredly was gratified and he was flattered, but he also was shocked, when headquarters insisted on giving him an honor guard of twenty-five men. He cried that Carl Vogel was enough for him (his chef already had quit, outraged by the rations he was expected to cook), and that those young fellows shouldn't be standing around looking stern—they should be cleaning weapons, doing guard duty, keeping up their own quarters, and most of all drilling, drilling, drilling. His protest, though it was vain, was loud. He kept on trying.

Chapter Twenty-seven

GENERAL ORDERS of Sunday, March 1, were largely hortatory, praising the soldiers for their endurance, urging them to further fortitude, and so forth; yet though they held no promise of amelioration, somehow they did seem to sigh, if faintly, in relief. February, that terrible February, had been surmounted.

Even so, winter held on, its grip tenacious; and the first thaw might make matters even worse, for the roads, frozen now, would be mud.

There were three principal reasons why the soldiers were being tortured: red tape, the failure of Congress to do anything about a successor to Thomas Mifflin, who had resigned as quartermaster general, and transportation.

Of these transportation was the worst.

Valley Forge had been selected for various reasons, among them its situation in the middle of a rich farming area. Yet for this very reason the countryside had been picked over by both armies, so that there was little of the edible left, while farmers had grown wary and cunning about hiding their goods. This meant that food for men and horses alike had to come from a long distance away—New Jersey, Maryland, Connecticut, Virginia. When the roads were mire, or all snow, it didn't come at all. Even when the roads were passable the delivery of supplies depended upon the army contractors, private parties, and even more upon the wagon drivers. Magazines, placed too close to streams, sometimes were washed away by freshets. It was not unusual for the driver, when hauling salted fish or meat, to stove in the tops of the barrels and pour off the brine. His object was to lighten his load. That he succeeded in spoiling the food didn't make any difference to him. All of the vehicles were unspeakably slow, and to avoid any encounter with British cutting-out parties they were required to take the long way around. Even so, some were overtaken, perhaps because of the activity of local loyalists: the last week in February, for instance, 130 head of cattle from Connecticut almost at the end of their trek, had been captured by British dragoons and driven to Philadelphia as the result of a tip from Bucks County, a hotbed of Tories.

Nevertheless, and unmistakably, hope was in the air. The cold couldn't last forever; and it was known in camp that the Commander in Chief was trying to persuade Nathanael Greene to take the position of quartermaster general.

Greene was reluctant. This should not be put down to coyness. He was hardheaded, of Quaker upbringing, a man with a family who could use a good-paying post. But like the Marquis de Lafayette, if with less noise, he sought glory; and who ever heard, he would ask, of a quartermaster general?

Nathanael Greene. *Courtesy New York Public Library Picture Collection*

Greene's wife, Catherine Littlefield Greene, and their baby were in camp now, as was plump Lucy Knox, daughter of a prominent loyalist family who had eloped from Boston with a bookseller who was now chief of the Continental artillery, and Lady Stirling, the major general's wife, with Lady Kitty, his daughter. There were times when headquarters was almost gay. Catherine Greene could manage a little French, and the French officers clustered around her whenever possible, drinking up each dear distorted word.

On Tuesday, March 10, an extra month's pay was issued to everybody in camp as a reward for having stuck it out all winter, and to this, unexpectedly—for the extra-month's-pay issue, having met a fight in Congress, was no secret—the Commander in Chief added a tot of rum per man.

The liquor situation had grown better. The third week in March there went out a summons for another conference on this subject, a conference which then set these prices for comparatively high-class beverages: gin, nine shillings a quart; West Indies rum, fifteen shillings; Continental rum, ten; French brandy, nineteen; "Cyder Royal," two.

News came of the arrival of a French ship at Portsmouth with huge supplies of clothing.

A few country people at last were induced to start a market within the purlieus of the camp; and even though they didn't have much to sell, there was, like a tingling bright promise in the air, the expectation of vegetables some time fairly soon.

Best of all, Greene at last agreed to be quartermaster general, provided he could have John Cox and Charles Pettit as assistants, and provided further that he would be assigned to lead the right wing in the next general engagement. To these terms, with an all but undignified haste, Congress and Washington assented. Greene was sworn in.

A week later Washington was approving of the new quartermaster general's proposal to post two-hundred-thousand-pound stacks of grain and forage along the Delaware north of Trenton, along the line from Valley Forge to Head of Elk, along the Schuylkill, and also along the line from Reading to Wright's

Ferry on the Susquehanna—this in order to be ready for pursuit in full strength whichever way the British moved when at last they did move. The wagon drivers? They had become quiet. Things were getting done.

At about this same time another Yankee, Colonel Jeremiah Wadsworth, was appointed commissary general. That department had been hobbled all winter by a quartermaster general's department that could not move goods. It was no longer so.

An order went out to check on the number and condition of all bayonets and spontoons.

There was singing again at Valley Forge.

Chapter Twenty-eight

THE CONTINENTAL soldier could move fast. He proved this time and again. Weedon and Muhlenberg took their brigades four miles in forty-five minutes at Brandywine, and started to fight immediately upon arrival. Greene's whole division went from the camp at Whitemarsh to Fort Mercer, thirty-five miles, in one day. Dan Morgan's deadly riflemen, a whole brigade, did it from Saratoga to Whitemarsh in eighteen days, averaging twelve miles a day, in late fall with full equipment.

This was in part because each Continental regiment carried so much less baggage than any British regiment, and was attended by fewer sutlers, laundresses, ammunition wives, etc.; and in part it could be accounted for by the fact that the Continental soldier, individually, carried little gear, at least as compared with the British soldier, who besides his uniform had to tote a sixty-pound pack, a musket that weighed fourteen pounds, a bayonet of somewhat more than one pound, and sixty rounds of ammunition.[90] The Hessian, even more heavily laden, could scarcely move.[91]

Certainly it was not because the Continentals knew how to march. They didn't—until Steuben taught them. There was no set pace in the American army, no measured stride. When Washington was issuing orders, Saturday, August 23, 1777, for the Philadelphia parade of the following day—orders that are touching in their anxious fuss—the best he could do about gait was to command that the drums and fifes should strike up and maintain "a time for the quick step . . . but with such moderation that the men may step to it with ease; and without dancing along."

Steuben selected and inculcated into the men a natural, easy, medium step. He started with a picked body of one hundred men from all parts of the army, temporarily attached to headquarters, and he taught them the step, as well as the manual of arms in only ten movements—a much simpler one than any in use in Europe. When these men knew what they were doing, he released them to teach others, and took on the instruction of another hundred. And so it went. Within a few weeks he had the whole army moving in much the same manner—in large masses too, for he was by then drilling regiments in the morning, whole brigades in the afternoon.

He gave lessons in mounting guard and in doing sentry duty. He inspected arms. He even introduced a central *time* into the Continental army with his requirement that all brigade majors every morning check their watches with the clock at headquarters. Each night he ran a school for adjutants. After that he settled down to do a stint on the first official U. S. Army drill book: "Regulations for the Order and Discipline of the Troops of the United States."[92]

This opus was produced page by page, painfully but with speed. Steuben wrote in French, which Duponceau promptly translated into English. The sheet then went to John Laurens and Alexander Hamilton, who "Americanized" it. Not until then was it passed around to the various brigade majors, each of whom copied it or caused it to be copied, before it went back to headquarters to be bound.

Thus sheet by sheet, paragraph by paragraph, almost word

by word, was the Continental army given, as it were, a constitution.

And still Steuben got up at dawn every day.

He taught the bayonet, something the Continental soldier badly needed. More and more long, sharp, triangular, ring-type bayonets were appearing in camp, from France; and Steuben taught how these should be carried at the left side, how they should be fastened to the musket at command, most important how they should be thrust. He taught this well, as the forthcoming battle of Monmouth was to prove. Until this time the bayonet had been used in the Continental army chiefly as a spit for cooking meat, or as a ground-breaker when there were trenches to be dug. Learning its correct use gave the soldier immeasurable confidence.

Since much of his earlier work must consist of *un*learning the troops, Steuben got Washington to issue an order forbidding the brigadiers to drill their men until further orders. This caused a great deal of grumbling, though until the arrival of Steuben there had been little enough zeal for drill on the part of the brigadiers who now were so indignant; but Washington upheld the foreigner.

It could be that Steuben's most telling contribution to the cause was his teaching the men to advance not in Indian file, as they had always done, but in columns of fours. This made for more speed, more immediate command by officers and non-coms, fewer stragglers, and deployment under battle conditions in less than half of the old time. American officers of course had considered this, but it had been dismissed as too difficult to teach. But Steuben taught it.

Had column-of-fours been the practice at Germantown it might have made all the difference. It *was* practiced thereafter in the Continental army. Redcoats, not redskins, were the immediate enemy.

The men were becoming proficient. They took more pride in their appearance. There was snap in the performance each morning when guard was mounted. Farmers came in from miles around to watch.

Through it all, and though his position remained anomalous —no actual rank, no salary, only a temporary assignment— Wilhelm Steuben stayed sunny. He liked to have company, and to share his drinks. Whenever he could get enough food he entertained at dinner, favoring generally the junior officers, for whom he felt sorry. They had field officers' stomachs, after all, he would say, field officers' appetites. Nor need they stand on their properness with him after parade hours. He could forgive a patch, a darn that showed, for he knew how it was. Once he even gave a dinner for junior officers to which none might have entry if his breeches were whole and unmended. He liked those lads, as he liked America itself.[93] Beaming, he called them his sans-culottes, thereby launching a word that soon afterward, across the sea, was to take on a more sinister meaning; but Steuben used it fondly.

Chapter Twenty-nine

THE BRIGHT young secretaries, who smelled *lèse-majesté* in anything less than a kowtow, were convinced that the whole Canadian expedition was a scheme to discredit George Washington, to weaken his central army, and to get Lafayette out of his hands and into those of Thomas Conway. Lafayette himself, distraught, loudly complaining, all but hysterical, soon came to think so too. It is likely that Washington, for all his calmness, and his reserve, entertained the same idea.

The expedition certainly was mismanaged from the beginning. And it was as certainly Horatio Gates's brain child, being in truth an extension of his earlier plan to have Stark knock out the British fleet in Lake Champlain. But that the choice was the Marquis de Lafayette for the command, with Conway as his second—De Kalb later was put into this post, Conway being shoved back to third place—in the circumstances was natural enough.

Something had to be done about those two. The Marquis outspokenly craved glory with a capital *G,* and he looked to Congress to give him a chance to get it. Washington still refused to grant him a command. He had the title of major general, but no men. He fumed.

As for Conway, he yet was a name in France, and a French alliance was the colonies' only road to victory. Benjamin Franklin and the others were working, over there in Paris. It might come through at any time, fetching the French fleet, which could win the war. Conway could be of no real service in the main army so long as Washington and certain others felt about him as they did; and if, disgruntled, he went back, moaning his woes, as he had threatened to do, this would not help.

Lafayette had had a few months of experience in summer army maneuvers in France, with the honorary rank of captain. It stood to reason that he needed a trained military man at his side; and Conway was that.

More important, the expedition was founded—as the first had been—on the assumption that the people of Canada would do practically anything to shake off the yoke of Britain. The Canadians had been granted terms unprecedented in their religious and political aspects, liberal beyond belief; but the thought in Congress was that they continued to hate England, and would fall in with any reasonable invader. Canada was not to be *conquered:* it was to be *liberated.* More than nine-tenths of its white inhabitants were Roman Catholics born in France or of French origin. Both Conway and Lafayette were Catholics. Lafayette was French. His English improved every day, but still had its faults. Conway, for all practical purposes, was as French as any Frenchman—he had lived in that country since boyhood—and talked both languages perfectly.

Conway had many enemies besides Washington. The brigadiers at Valley Forge despised him. He had sneered at them. He had jumped over their heads to be made a major general. And he was anti-Washington.

They made up an earnest, determined, dedicated lot, those

brigadier generals. They were not always admirable in their personal habits, certainly not all of them were gentlemen, and they were a quarrelsome, jealous pack, inordinately concerned with rank and precedent, unsure of themselves in strange uniforms, and bound that they wouldn't take sass from any outsider. One and all—"Big John" Paterson, Enoch Poor the shipbuilder, Ebenezer Learned, Jim Potter, the forthright, pushingly plain-spoken Charles Scott, "Scotch Willie" Maxwell, John Peter Gabriel Muhlenberg the pastor—they were devoted to their Commander in Chief. "Next to God Almighty and my country, I revere General Washington," Varnum wrote to a friend, "and nothing fills me with so much indignation as the villainy of some who dare speak disrespectfully of him."[94] They were not fools and not fanatics, and if they lacked that worldliness sometimes thought of as requisite for a general, they could work hard and long—and intelligently.

They were young. Knox was twenty-seven, Varnum twenty-nine, Pulaski thirty, Wayne thirty-four, Cadwalader thirty-six. We do not have all the birth figures, but their mean age could hardly have been much above forty.

None of the brigadiers could "call out" Thomas Conway, who was a major general, but there is little doubt that many if not most of them, given the chance, would have done so.

Congress thought of an exit. To soothe Lafayette's ruffled aristocratic feelings—since the abandonment of the Canadian enterprise now seemed all but certain—Congress adopted a resolution mightily praising him for his efforts. Two days later the president of that body, Laurens, wrote the Marquis a personal letter assuring him that this resolution was wholehearted, not simply a matter of form.

March 13, Congress voted to suspend the attack on Canada, and to authorize George Washington to recall Lafayette and De Kalb, nothing being said about Conway.

Now of a sudden the whole project, Gates's, which until a little while ago was heartily supported from the floor, became unmentionable. "Except my own, I do not remember three dissenting voices," Laurens wrote to his friend John Rutledge,

March 11. "Now—well, 'I never liked that Canadian Expedition' is unanimous." He added, in a masterpiece of understatement, that Lafayette "is seriously chagrined with the planners of that amusement."

Back in his quarters on the Berwyn road, just outside of the Valley Forge camp, Lafayette could no longer be denied. He was given his division. It consisted of three brigades—Muhlenberg's, Scott's, and Woodford's—eleven regiments, totaling 3,086 men, all Virginians.

Conway, stranded, spluttered. At last he sent in his resignation, which Congress instantly accepted.

Conway then wrote that he had not *meant* to resign. Congress had *misunderstood* him.

Congress, by a vote of twenty-three to four, without comment, placed this protest upon the table, from which it was never lifted. Then, at Washington's recommendation and with an alacrity all but insulting, Congress made Wilhelm Steuben a major general and the inspector general of the Continental army.

Conway, without rank or any position, came down from Albany to York and argued and cajoled, but there was no further action from the floor. "The door is shut," Laurens said.

It gave the brigadiers their chance. Conway now was a civilian. John Cadwalader got him out on the field of honor.

Conway missed. Cadwalader's bullet clacked through Conway's teeth and smashed all his lower jaw; he fell, fountaining blood.

"Well, I've stopped that damn' lying mouth for a while," said Brigadier General John Cadwalader.

It appeared to most that he had stopped it for good. Conway lay abed a long time, expecting to die. One day—it was July 23, 1778—he wrote to George Washington.

"Sir: I find myself just able to hold the pen during a few minutes, and take this opportunity of expressing my sincere grief for having done, written, or said anything disagreeable to your Excellency. My career will soon be over; therefore justice and truth prompt me to declare my last sentiments. You are in my eyes the great and good man. May you long enjoy the love, veneration, and esteem of those States, whose liberties you have asserted by your virtues. I am with the greatest respect, etc. Thomas Conway."

Lacking a sense of the dramatic, he didn't die. He drifted back to France—and obscurity. George Washington by that time had other things to think about.

Chapter Thirty

April at Valley Forge was marked by two miracles.

Even to those who had lived along the Delaware, the Hudson, the Connecticut, there was something amazing every spring when the shad began to run. It was so abrupt, so violent, and seemingly senseless! No doubt those fish were answering an instinct that bade them hasten up a fresh-water stream and lay their eggs; but the tale of the Yankee Bogle, a mythical bird which, squawking, led them upriver, in truth is easier to believe; for while nobody ever had seen that creature it was sure that the maddened upsurging shad appeared to be hypnotized, fascinated, entoiled in some melody no others could hear, blindly following some avian or piscatorial Pied Piper.

When the shad came as far up the Schuylkill (from out of the Delaware) as Valley Forge, that meant a big run. Thanks to local men, the Continental army was prepared for it. The spring rises had not yet started; the river ran shallow, and it was possible for cavalrymen to ride right up the middle of it, almost knee-to-knee. Each carried a cut bush with which he beat the water. At the narrowest point, Pawling's Ford, just outside of camp a little north of headquarters, where the Perkiomen Creek emptied into the Schuylkill, nets had been spread.

The fish swam in, got caught by the gills, and couldn't get

back. There were thousands of them, more and more coming all day, every day, all night too, for weeks.

Shad was not looked upon as a luxury but rather was a poor man's fish. There had been clauses in the contracts of indentured servants providing that they must not be fed shad more than twice a week, and the roe was thrown away. But it was good enough for the Continentals, who gorged on it.

For almost a month the whole camp stank, and men's fingers were oily. In addition, barrels had been held in readiness, and hundreds of these were filled with salted shad for future consumption.

The second miracle, which occurred somewhat later that month, satisfied the soul rather than the stomach.

On a certain morning, the date of which is not recorded, the troopers tumbled out at reveille for breakfast and for drill—to find the world around them white with dogwood blossoms.

There is nothing gradual about these. They appear all at once, everywhere, as though at a signal, as though word had been passed along the edge of the oak forests in the shadow of which they grow.

The dogwood, a tough small tree more like a bush, is inconspicuous and even drab throughout most of the year; but in the autumn its leaves take on a dark rich red, a sumac-like crimson, almost as lovely as poison ivy; and in the spring, as though all the trees had got together the night before and carefully rehearsed, it bursts out into huge, spectacular white blossoms, millions of them: it fairly *smashes* upon the sight. Before, it had been hard to find. Now (if anyone wished to do so) it would be difficult to avoid. For several weeks those blossoms own the world in which the people who see them are so lucky to live.[95]

If any of the British foraging parties ventured that far out into the country during those gorgeous weeks, their members too must have stood astounded. There is no dogwood like that in England. There is only, in the southern parts, *Cornus sanguinea,* as compared with the American *Cornus florida. Cornus sanguinea* features the same dark red leaves in autumn, but its spring flowers, though white, are small, dull, even mean, and it was valued not as a piece of decoration but because for many years its bark was thought to be a cure for mange—hence, according to some authorities, the name "dogwood"—while in America, at the same time, the Indians, who had no dogs, were mixing that bark with their tobacco; nobody knows why.

Thus it might have been impressed upon some of the invaders that the damned rebels had *two* points of superiority—their flints and their dogwood.

For all the drill and the rain, there was an air of blithesomeness at Valley Forge. You couldn't quench men like that. Free of those fires with their acrid smoke, they got out more, got around. They played long bullets, a bowling game for which they used cannonballs in a corner of the parade. They played rounders, a recent import from England; and this might have been the first time that baseball was practiced in the United States, baseball being the direct descendant of rounders. The Commander in Chief himself—and the word went around the camp like heat lightning—for a little while one afternoon diverted himself with a game of "wickets."

The least superstitious of the soldiers could hardly fail to be affected by those two signs, the shad and the dogwood. Something good was going to happen.

Something good did.

Militiamen were filtering in, reinforcements in preparation for the spring campaign. On May 1, it was estimated that there were 11,500 soldiers and officers at Valley Forge—the most yet, despite desertion and sickness. That same day Maypoles were erected, songs sung, and every soldier wore flowers in his hat—in honor, it was said, of King Tammany, sometimes called "St. Tammany," the Leni-Lenape chief who was to give his name (in the Delaware language it means "the Affable") to a certain political organization. It was a local custom, and everybody was having a good time. Some of the men serenaded Washington at headquarters, but he didn't appear though he sent out word to thank them. The reason he did not come forth was not indisposition. The reason was that he had just heard the news and, not wishing it to be announced until it had been confirmed, feared that his face might show the joy he felt.

A courier had brought it, unofficially, from the headquarters of Major General Alexander McDougall at Fishkill, New York. It seems that Simeon Deane, a brother of Silas Deane, lately landed, had just passed through Fishkill on his way to York to make known the news formally to Congress. The courier had ridden ahead of him.

It was the best news that could possibly have come.

France had joined the war.

Chapter Thirty-one

THERE IS many a truth spoken in seriousness. The Marquis de Lafayette had no sense of humor, and when, having heard that Howe had asked to be relieved and was being recalled, he remarked to young Laurens that the general's departure would be a great loss to the United States, he meant just that. And he was right.

Conditions in Philadelphia were somewhat better than they had been at first, and the terrible inflation caused by the siege—for it still was a siege—had abated a bit. Yet prices remained two to three times what they were in the market at Valley Forge, and nobody was happy about this. Perhaps it was just as well that General Howe should go home.

To impugn the courage of a professional soldier is senseless. Theoretically at least, the general of any army thinks not of his own physical peril but that of his men.

History, however, has been hard put to find any excuse for Sir William Howe, who never did rise from that bed to grasp the warlike spear. Mrs. L. alone, dazzling though she might have been, could hardly make up the whole answer.

The man was by nature amiable, and in his politics a Whig. When first he came to this country it was with not only an army but authority, together with his brother the Admiral, to treat for peace. He seems always to have fancied himself in that capacity, as a mediator rather than a conqueror. In Philadelphia, now, he knew that fresh peace commissioners were on the way, and his orders were to work with them. He knew, too, that he was to be succeeded by his general commanding New York, Henry Clinton, lately knighted, who himself was to be one of the commissioners. In the circumstances it would be wasted effort to threaten a fortified camp like Valley Forge.

It would not have been wasted effort earlier. Yet Sir William had not given so much as a growl in that direction.

There is another possible explanation. More than one puzzled historian has advanced the suggestion that Howe had been awed, even terrified, certainly greatly moved by the carnage in the battle for Bunker Hill, where blood was so heavily splashed upon him. Called upon by the Commons to explain his inactivity in Philadelphia, he was to testify that he had sent engineers to study the Continental position, and that they reported that it could only be taken by a frontal attack—at terrible expense.

Had he been overeager about accepting that report? Did he still see hideously mutilated men spinning and falling all around him, while his gaiters were reddened to the knee? Did the shrieks of the hit ring in his ears months afterwards, and could this have been why he so frequently consulted the bottle?

If so, that argued no diminution of his mettle. He might have been asking himself whether indeed the European military method was 100 per cent right, the American lack of method 100 per cent wrong. For a long time now professionals had been assuring the Continental troops that they could never win by staying behind things, that they must get out in the open and beat the enemy at his own game. Was it conceivable that now the commander of the British was having qualms? Did it occur to him that perhaps *his* men could never win unless they were taught sometimes to take cover?

If so, he did nothing about it. Not for him the embarrassments and frustrations of the innovator. He had tried the old accepted practices, and he'd failed. He was going back. He was glad of it.

His officers, who loved him, were not; nor yet were the men, who knew they would not have an easy time under Clinton.

The officers decided to send him off in style; and the farewell party they planned, May 18, 1778, though it was in honor of a failure among failures, was proportionately as expensive as any triumph in the decadent days of Rome. Caesar himself, Germanicus, Belisarius, had hardly been so exuberantly and elaborately cheered.

True, there were no silver cages of beasts from Africa. There were no slaughterings in the Colosseum. There weren't any pagan emperors, dragging their chains, to spit upon. It would hardly have done to bring in Commissioner Loring's charges, for most of them had been so starved that they could scarcely stand, much less march. But with what material they had, the officers, masterminded by the ineffable André, did wonders. Such a spectacle had never before been seen over here.

It was called the Mischianza, which is Italian for "medley," and it was a *fête champêtre* in form, preceded by a regatta, followed by a "tournament" that was not unlike the entertainments Queen Elizabeth I would have been regaled with while on progress two and a half centuries before, though Elizabeth would have giggled at this one.

It started on the river, with cannonading and all sorts of salutes from ship and shore alike.

The barges were drawn up at the site of the festivities, the Wharton place, Walnut Grove (there is a Pennsylvania Railroad station there now), and the hero stepped out to be greeted with a fanfare of trumpets. After that an elaborately got-up herald read him a Latin ode in praise of his warlike prowess. Sir William didn't understand a word of Latin, but he could smile and nod, and did.

The party then proceeded with pomp under two plaster arches painted like marble to the "lists."

(At about this time Alan McLane raided the suburbs; but the stroke had been anticipated, and not all the soldiery were drawn up at Walnut Grove, so that before he could do much damage he and his men were chased to the cover of the Wissahickon Hills.)

If there were no prisoners in the parade or in the regatta, there were some, theoretically at least, at the "lists." Fourteen of Philadelphia's fairest girls, carefully selected, were gathered there, and they were dressed à la Turk, in spangled turbans and white silk dresses and sashes ordered from London, the firm of Coffin & Anderson.

It is sometimes said that Peggy Shippen, she who soon afterward married Benedict Arnold, was one of the lucky fourteen, and that at the Mischianza she danced with Major André. She must have danced with André many times in Philadelphia that winter, for he was an extremely prominent young man and fond of the girls, but she was not at the Mischianza. She had been invited to be one of the immortal "captives;" but her father, a Quaker, perhaps because he disapproved of Turkish costumes, perhaps for other reasons, had forbidden it. Peggy stayed home, doubtless in tears, for she too had "caught scarlet fever."

Now the Knights of the Blended Rose rode forth, seven of them, each on a white horse, each carrying a wooden shield upon which had been emblazoned two white roses twisted together at the stems, with, underneath: "We droop when separated."

The leader of this band then made a public statement, viz., "The Knights of the Blended Rose, by me their Herald, proclaim and assert that the Ladies of the Blended Rose excel in wit, beauty, and every accomplishment, those of the *whole World;* and, should any Knight or Knights be so hardy as to dispute or deny it, they are ready to enter the lists with them, and maintain their assertions by deeds of arms, according to the laws of ancient chivalry."

This was more than the Knights of the Burning Mountain could stand. Seven in number, they were garbed in orange and black, and they rode black horses, and each carried a shield on which there was a picture of a volcano, and under it: "I burn for ever."

So the Knights of the Burning Mountain then proclaimed, through their Herald, that *their* ladies excelled in wit, beauty, etc., all others in the world; and after some more of this it was decided to fight with lances and swords. They had rehearsed it well, and nobody was hurt. The contest was halted, thrillingly, when all fourteen of the Turkish captives, joining hands, declared in verse that all fourteen of the knights were equally valiant and bold, and that they, the captives, entreated them in the name of love to fight no more. Then everybody sat down to dinner; and afterward there was dancing and fireworks until midnight, while the privates and non-coms were given an extra ration of rum.[96]

Long before that the boys at Valley Forge were in their blankets.

Chapter Thirty-two

A FEU DE JOIE, a sort of whole-army salute, a salute of many muskets, was a difficult thing to execute. It called for discipline, good timing, a minimum of misfires. It also called for a great deal of gunpowder; but there was gunpowder at Valley Forge the morning of May 6, 1778. There was plenty of everything there, even vegetables. Philadelphia remained under siege; and though the original inflationary prices had been modified, city market conditions were not as good as they were on that grim hillside: butter at Valley Forge sold at three shillings sixpence a pound, while in Philadelphia it cost seven shillings; potatoes, sixteen shillings a bushel in the city, fetched only ten at camp; veal was four shillings in one place, tenpence in the other.

A *feu de joie* should celebrate some great and happy event.

The one at Valley Forge was ordered, of course, because of the French alliance, the news by that time being official, confirmed.

There had been an earlier salute, which could hardly have been joyous and certainly was not well performed, at the camp in the Gulph, just before the bloody-footed march to Valley Forge. That had been for the purpose of celebrating the Continental victory at Saratoga. There had been no parade in the Gulph, and after the shooting, which was ragged, and a formal cheer, the chaplains had addressed the men, who, scarcely able to stand, did not respond with glee.

It was different now. The dogwood was in bloom, the air balmy, and the men marched with snap. Each looking spruce, whether officer or private, with a bit of greenery stuck into his hat, they formed in two lines facing each other, double rank, and started the *feu de joie* . . . one gun after another, from right to left along the front line . . . then from left to right along the second line.

It went off perfectly.

The official announcement of the alliance was read, and there was a cheer. It was made known that in honor of the occasion a gill of rum would be dealt out to each man, and there was another cheer. Steuben, who must have been the proudest person in all that army just then as he watched the nicely moving men, at last was given his major general's commission.

There was a drill, a parade-past. The sun shone on cockades, bayonets, pipe-clayed belts, boots.

Afterward the rum was served, while officers and ladies sat down to a meal. It would have been thought mean in Philadelphia; but no festivity there, no matter what it cost, could have exceeded this in good spirits.

Anyway, the British were not likely to be in Philadelphia much longer. Word came from spies the middle of May that they were undoubtedly preparing to depart. This had been expected ever since the news of the French alliance. Clinton, who would soon be in command, could not risk being bottled up in Philadelphia by the French. By losing unchallenged control of the seacoast the British were losing almost everything. Clinton had about ten thousand men in Philadelphia, about four thousand in New York, two thousand in Rhode Island. He must bring these together lest they be knocked out separately by the boys from Valley Forge; for he could not immediately expect reinforcements. New York was the logical place to do this. But—would he move by ship, risking encounter with a French fleet that might even then be making for America? Or would he attack the Continentals in their camp? They were ready for that. It was believed that he would head for New York by land, across New Jersey. If this happened, the Continentals—their generals already had decided it—would go right after him, hitting him.

But *until* Clinton moved there was nothing for the Continental army to do but sharpen weapons and enjoy the spring weather.

Clinton, who had been appointed one of the peace commissioners, already was in Philadelphia, where he had the honor of attending the Mischianza and listening to that long Latin speech. Clinton had no Mrs. L. and was not sunk in sloth; but he had been left to hold a sick baby.

On June 6, the other peace commissioners, Lord Howe, Lord Carlyle, and Sir William Eden, arrived. It had been a long trip, for nothing. They brought news that every one of the enactments the American colonists found objectionable had been repealed. Great Britain would give in on every point save one. The colonies must discard their pretensions to independent statehood. They must pay at least a nominal allegiance to the Crown.

Congress did not even listen, didn't consent so much as to receive the commissioners. Nothing less than full independence would be considered. There wasn't a debate; there was not a single dissenting vote.

Howe went back. The peace commissioners went back. On June 18, early, Clinton crossed the Delaware and started for Sandy Hook.

At the junction of the Valley Creek and the Schuylkill River,

Deborah Hewes was thanked for the use of her small stone house, and was paid one hundred pounds, Pennsylvania currency, as six months' rent. Washington had packed. So had the rest of the army.

Next morning, with a swinging step, drums beating, fifes loud, the men started for New Jersey—and the British. They were ready to fight.

They left behind them only entrenchments, huts, breastworks, charred stumps of their fires, trampled grass—and an imperishable memory.

Notes

1. Adams, *Familiar Letters,* p. 298.

2. "In 1774 a Philadelphian wrote to a member of parliament that there were sufficient gun makers in the Colonies to make 100,000 stand of muskets per year at 28 shillings each, and powder was already made. Yet, although the Revolution was imminent, and the need of a store of firearms apparent, the home consumption was such that the outbreak of hostilities found the Colonists poorly provided. This negligence on the part of the Colonists seems inexcusable. For more than a year the outbreak of hostilities was expected daily. Committees of correspondence had been active, and a union of the thirteen Colonies against the mother country was assured; there was no national government, no executive, yet each Colony for self-protection should have established armories–and did not." Sawyer, *Firearms in American History,* p. 71.

3. The only uniformed troops on the Continental side at the battle for Bunker's Hill were those of Captain John Chester's company from Wethersfield, Conn. These were so conspicuous in their blue-turned-over-with-red coats that before the fighting started they prudently covered them with hunting shirts. Gardner, *Uniforms of the American Army;* Lefferts, *Uniforms,* etc.; Fitzpatrick, *The Continental Army Uniform;* Ogden, *Uniform of the Army of the United States.*

4. Fitzpatrick, *The Spirit of the Revolution,* pp. 158-78; Curtis, *Organization of the British Army,* p 8.

5. Oddly, Mahan appears to class him with Rodney, Keppel, St. Vincent. *Influence of Sea Power,* pp. 9, 500. In his subsequent *Major Operations of the Navies in the War of American Independence,* perhaps because it was written to form part of a history of the British Navy, Mahan remained at least not censorious. An Englishman is less forgiving: Fortescue, *History of the British Army,* vol. III, p. 212. The British point of view is also expressed in Anderson's *Command of the Howe Brothers,* pp. 221-26. "The utter failure of the two Howes to avail themselves of the sea power by instituting a rigid blockade of the

Chesapeake and Delaware bays can be explained only on grounds of professional incapacity. They neither of them knew how to make effective use of the weapon at their command." Adams, *Studies Military and Diplomatic,* p. 122. See also Knox, *Naval Genius of George Washington,* pp. 34-8

6. Yet in France, Germantown was hailed as a victory, veritably a triumph, proof yet again that the Continental could hold his own and more, given half a chance. This could be in part because the news arrived at the same time as did the news of the battle of Saratoga, which had occurred only a few days later. For whatever reason, Germantown did much to influence the French to declare war; and there is evidence that even at home, once men had begun to ponder it, it was accepted as a good rather than bad sign. As one historian says, at Germantown Washington "had inflicted upon them [the British] one of those victories which in the end cost them the war." Gottschalk, *Lafayette Joins the American Army,* p. 60.

7. Burnett, *Letters of Members of the Continental Congress,* vol. II, p 594.

8. Fitzpatrick, *George Washington Himself,* pp. 318-23.

9. Worthington C. Ford in his article, "The Defenses of Philadelphia," in the *Pennsylvania Magazine of History and Biography* (vols. XIX, XX, and XXI), sets forth in full all of these opinions. They are worth reading.

10. The loot (which was of course legitimate) included candles, soap, 25 barrels of horseshoes, 20 hogsheads of rum, 3,800 barrels of flour, and several thousand tomahawks and kettles, also some "intrenching tools." Montresor, *Journals,* pp. 454-56.

11. Fitzpatrick, *Writings,* vol. X, pp. 470-71.

12. It was relocated, the following year, at the mouth of the creek, where it turned out metal goods for the rest of the Revolution; but the original forge was in ruins, as it yet is today.

13. Originally the plant itself had been called the Mount Joy Forge. Nobody knows why or just when the name was changed.

14. From York, Pa., May 16, 1778. *Complete Works,* vol. II, p. 285.

15. *Writings,* vol. XI, p. 286. Again, in a report to the Committee of Congress with the Army, January 29, 1778: "A small knowledge of human nature will convince us, that, with far the greatest part of mankind, interest is the governing principle; and that almost every man is more or less, under its influence. Motives of public virtue may for a time, or in particular instances, actuate men to the observance of a conduct purely disinterested; but they are not of themselves sufficient to produce a persevering conformity to the refined dictates and obligations of social duty. Few men are capable of making a continual sacrifice of all views of private interest, or advantage, to the common good. It is vain to exclaim against the depravity of human nature on this account; the fact is so, the experience of every age and nation has proved it and we must in great measure, change the constitution of man, before we can make it otherwise. No institution, not built on the presumptive truth of these maxims can succeed." *Writings,* vol. X, p. 363.

16. Wade and Lively, *This Glorious Cause,* p. 118.

17. "The inscription on his tombstone in Lebanon truly recites that 'he fell a victim' to the 'perpetual cares and fatigues' of his office. His toilsome career was inconspicuous and soon forgotten, but he died for his country as truly and heroically as the soldier who falls in the forefront of battle." Trumbull, *Jonathan Trumbull,* pp. 171-72. He was forty-two years old. The best account of the supply system is in Hatch's *Administration of the American Revolutionary Army,* chapter 5.

18. Greene, vol. I, p. 543.

19. *Correspondence,* p. 126.

20. Roosevelt, *Gouverneur Morris,* p. 78. "What a lot of damned scoundrels we had in that Second Congress," Morris was to write later to John Jay, who replied, "Yes, we had." Swiggett, *The Extraordinary Mr. Morris,* p. 42.

21. Officially the currency of the country still was expressed in pounds, shillings, and pence, but in fact many persons

thought and spoke in terms of dollars. This was not a U. S. dollar but the Spanish eight-real piece (Long John Silver's parrot's "pieces of eight") which was very common in the colonies, particularly the seaports, because of our trade, much of which was illicit, with the Spanish West Indies. Congress, as here, customarily expressed money in terms of the dollar, spelling it out, for the symbol $ had not yet been devised. Oddly, the word itself comes from Germany, being a modification of *thaler* (itself a shortening of *Joachimsthaler),* in the sixteenth century a coin made of silver from the newly discovered mine in Joachimsthal (Joachim's Dale), Bohemia.

22. Belcher, *First American Civil War,* vol. II, p. 5.

23. The high-strung Hamilton was to squabble with Washington and quit, much later; but this was quickly mended. Schachner, *Alexander Hamilton,* pp. 120-24.

24. Rawle, *Sketch of the Life of Thomas Mifflin.*

25. "Friends of the Commander-in-chief, blinded by their love for him who to their eyes could do no wrong, saw the board 'packed' with his enemies, an instrument of cabal. Forgotten were the innocent circumstances under which the board was established." Roseman, *Thomas Mifflin and the Politics of the American Revolution,* p. 114.

26. These were the first free-floating mines in history. They soon came to be called torpedos; and when Farragut at Mobile Bay shouted "Damn the torpedos! Go ahead!" these were what he meant, not the cigar-shaped "tin fish" of today. "Torpedo" (Latin for stiffness, numbers) first was applied to the electric ray, a fish. The reader will note the similarity between Bushnell's plan and Winston Churchill's early in World War II when he proposed to drop by plane into the upper Rhine large numbers of floating mines that would explode on contact.

27. Copyright laws did not exist, and it was the custom to pirate any tune that the public seemed to like. In view of its spread, the origin of "Yankee Doodle" is curiously misted. The melody had been known for some time before the Revolution. It appears to have been a folk air. Articles—some learned, some simply pretentious, none listed here—have been written to

prove that it was of Hungarian, Persian, German, Scottish, Irish, English, Catalonian, and even Turkish origin. In 1907 the late O. G. Sonneck, at that time chief of the music division of the Library of Congress, was assigned to make some sense out of all this, and also out of the conflicting stories that concern the beginnings of "The Star-Spangled Banner," "America," and "Hail Columbia." His report (see SOURCES) is the best there is of "Yankee Doodle." He lists seventeen separate theories, and believes that every one of them is wrong. The first words written under this title, "Yankee Doodle," might have been by an English surgeon in Braddock's army of 1754, or by another Englishman in Amherst's army a year or two later. It doesn't matter. Both mock the oaf who gawped, goggle-eyed, at a proper army camp. The redcoats stationed in and near Boston used to stand outside of churches on Sunday mornings when services were in progress, and howl "Yankee Doodle" at the top of their lungs. Taunted, the Continentals took it up and tossed it back, glorying in the name, making it their own. Yet the very name itself remains a mystery. The "Doodle" is easy. It might have been onomatopoeic or just silly, as refrain words in topical ballads so often were; or conceivably, as Johnson has it in his *Dictionary,* a contraction of "do" and "little"; or again it could once have been "tootle," for "Yankee Doodle" was what was called a "flute song." The word, too, had long been familiar as that for a clown: Doodle and Noodle were a comic pair, excessively maladroit, in many Restoration plays. But over "Yankee" professors have fought and will fight. ". . . this impertinent, jolly little tune has thumbed its nose at many a dignified sage, and grayed hundreds of hairs by hiding its origin." (Howard, *Our American Music,* p. 117.) Some say that it is an Indian corruption of the word "English" through "Yengees" to "Yankees"; some that it came from the Cherokee word "eankke," meaning coward or slave, bestowed by colonial Virginians upon the New Englanders when the latter refused to help fight the Cherokees; others that it was an adjective often used to mean "good" or "excellent" by Jonathan Hastings, a well-liked farmer of Cambridge, Massachusetts, *circa* 1713; still others that it came from the Dutch diminutive of "Jan," that is, "Janke," or a folding-together of Jan and Kees, which is to say "John Cheese"—in either case being a derisive nickname the original settlers of New Amsterdam gave their neighbors the original settlers of Connecticut. The last is the theory seemingly favored by the *Oxford English Dictionary,* the *Dictionary of American English,* and the late H. L. Mencken (*The American Language,* supplement I, pp. 192-97); but there are many others.

28. She even trailed him back to England, where, he being married, she turned respectable; and her son (by Loring) became the first Archdeacon of Calcutta. Blumenthal, *Camp Followers,* pp. 34-6.

29. "To the cause of the Revolution, it was perhaps worth as much, just then, by way of emotional tonic and of military inspiration, as the winning of a considerable battle would have been." Tyler, *Literary History of the American Revolution,* vol. II, p. 149.

30. A brigadier at Valley Forge, Knox was to become a major general and our first secretary of war. Of the three biographies of him—Brooks's, Drake's, and Callahan's (see SOURCES)—the last, which is the latest, is the best.

31. Wade and Lively, *This Glorious Cause,* p. 118.

32. Three of the piers and most of the planking were torn away by floe-clogged water the following January, and the rest in time simply fell apart. It was never rebuilt.

33. Baurmeister, *Letters and Journals,* p. 145.

34. Kapp, *Life of John Kalb,* pp. 141-42.

35. *Writings,* (Ford edition) vol. 4, p. 441. "Added to the discouragements attendant upon this conglomerate mass of men, which resembled in discipline, uniform and organization more nearly a Greek ekklesia than an army, was the low type of commissioned officer." Ganoe, *History of the United States Army,* p. 4.

36. In contrast, drunkenness was a curse in the British army. Between June 1, 1778, and June 31, 1781, £359,573 was paid out from the British commissary in America for 1,595,775

gallons of rum (a generic name for any high-content alcoholic spirits), though there must also have been a great deal that was bootlegged. This is three times what was paid out over this same period for beef, pork, bread, and flour combined. Blumenthal, *Camp Followers,* p. 24.

37. *Diary,* p. 158.

38. Bezanson and associates, *Prices and Inflation . . . Pennsylvania, 1770-90, passim.*

39. Masefield, *Sea Life in Nelson's Time,* p. 165.

40. "The plot which has passed into history as the Conway Cabal originated some time before Conway had anything to do with it, and was in its nature political rather than military." Ford, *Defences of Philadelphia,* p. 90.

41. Perkins, *France in the American Revolution,* p. 96.

42. "Commissary-General Blanchard, of the French Army, relates that when he dined with General Varnum at his pleasant home, in August, 1780, their conversation was in Latin." Gardiner, "Varnum," *Magazine of American History,* XVIII, 1887, pp. 185-93.

43. *Writings,* letter dated January 2, 1778.

44. Ganoe, *History of the United States Army,* p. 56.

45. "Gates was the military idol of the day. He had actually compelled the surrender of an entire British army, and that was a pedestal large enough to sustain a popular hero. The fact that Gates had had four times as many men as Burgoyne was not taken into account; nor was the fact that the British at Saratoga were out of food and hopelessly lost in the woods. They would have surrendered if Gates had been in China." Woodward, *George Washington,* p. 336.

46. Burnett, *The Continental Congress,* p. 271.

47. Waldo, *Diary.*

48. *Memoirs,* vol. I, p. 331.

49. The subject of the Conway Cabal has fascinated historians, who are agreed on only one thing about it—that it shouldn't have been called after Conway: the pull of alliteration might account for this. Earlier writers, exalting Washington as was the custom, quite naturally blackened the name of

anybody who ever breathed a doubt of Washington's ability as a general. This, the dramatic method, calls for a villain. More recently there have risen doubts as to whether there really was any organized plot to unseat the Commander in Chief, whether it wasn't just a pool of discontented mutterings. Burnett (*The Continental Congress,* p. 279) wonders whether it should be called an intrigue, a conspiracy, or a cabal, finally—though not at all in the manner of one who has convinced himself—plumping for the last. Alden (*The American Revolution,* pp. 198-99) handles the subject gingerly, while Butterfield (*Letters of Benjamin Rush,* vol. II, Appendix I) all but concludes that there wasn't any such thing. ". . . The basic cause of the quarrel stands out clearly: Rush was given to reckless criticism, and Washington was extremely sensitive to any kind of criticism." Here (p. 1197) he means the quarrel between Washington and his surgeon general; but the same thing could be said of John Adams, Samuel Adams, Richard Henry Lee, Thomas Conway, Thomas Mifflin, and sundry others. The best discussion of this is contained in Bernhard Knollenberg's *Washington and the Revolution: A Reappraisal, chapter* VII. His conclusion is, in effect, that no manner of plot existed, not even a loose understanding-in-opposition. The book was published in 1940; but though Mr. Knollenberg is presently preparing a second edition, he will make no substantial change in this much-discussed chapter.

50. His biographer credits him with three months at Valley Forge, implying that he bunked among the men (Rowland, *Charles Carroll of Carrolton,* vol. I, pp. 235-6). But Burnett (*The Continental Congress,* p. 298) says he never went to camp at all.

51. *Journals and Letters,* p. 145.

52. "The doctrines of the Quakers were democratic to the core, emphasizing brotherly love, mutual aid and comfort, pacifism, justice for all on equal terms, rejection of priestly authority, and complete religious individualism. The good Quaker, whe centered his worldly thoughts upon the problems of individual conduct, would have denied that he possessed any particular theories of state and government. Yet since de-

mocracy is simply the presence of a certain number of democrats, and since the good democrat believes in principles that the Quakers put first in their catalogue of virtues, it is plain that the teachings of this sect gave substance to the growing theory of political liberty." Rossiter, *Seedtime of the Republic,* p. 48. See also Boorstin, *The Americans,* pp. 33-69.

53. Scott, *Counterfeiting in Colonial America,* pp. 12, 253.

54. Greene, I, 533. Stewart, *Foraging for Valley Forge,* pp. 144-64.

55. *Correspondence,* pp. 108-9.

56. Clark, chapter I; Stedman I, 387. Throughout the seven years of the active American Revolution, between Lexington and Yorktown, out of a population of more than three millions scarcely fifty thousand were ever at one time under arms in defense of freedom. ". . . while, by way of contrast, the student of history may notice that in the War of Secession the six millions of the Southern States put 400,000 men into the field in defense of the Peculiar Institution." Belcher, *First American Civil War,* I, 73.

57. *Journals and Letters,* p. 150.

58. Perhaps the best description of those days is contained in Sargent's life of André (see SOURCES), chapters X and XI. But see also Anderson, *Command of the Howe Brothers,* chap. XVI.

59. The game is still popular there, the only place in this country where it has aroused any notable interest.

60. *Diary,* pp. 40-1.

61. It is undated, but Fitzpatrick places it at about January 30. *Writings,* vol. X, pp. 405-7.

62. Jordan, "Military Hospitals," *Pennsylvania Magazine of History and Biography,* vol. XX, no. 2.

63. Zinsser, *Rats, Lice and History, passim.*

64. Belcher, *The First American Civil War,* vol. I, pp. 257-58.

65. Burnett, vol. III, p. 154.

66. Kite, *Duportail,* chapter 2, is the best description of the defense engineering work at Valley Forge.

67. Sweet, *Religion in Colonial America,* p. 66. See also Manross, *American Episcopal Church;* Thornton, *Pulpit of the American Revolution;* Cross, *Anglican Episcopate in the American Colonies;* Van Tyne, *Influence of the Clergy,* etc.

68. Vivacious, audacious, supremely mendacious Parson Weems started that story about a Quaker, Isaac Potts, who encountered Washington on his knees in a grove of oak near Valley Forge. Like Weems's cherry-tree tale, this caught on. It has been commemorated in a plaque on the U. S. Sub-Treasury building in New York, on millions of two-cent stamps, and on the walls of half the schoolrooms in the country. When Rupert Hughes *(George Washington,* vol. III, chapter XXI, pp. 270-298) tore it to shreds, pointing out that Potts didn't own that land then and probably was in Philadelphia anyway, that there was little snow in Valley Forge in 1777-78 but a great deal of rain and of course mountains of mud, and that Washington had a perfectly dry house in which to pray, there was a certain stir. However, professional historians, who had known this all along, were not shocked.

69. G. W. Greene, *Nathanael Greene,* vol. I, p. 131.

70. Kapp, *John Kalb,* p. 127.

71. Greene, vol. I, p. 417.

72. *Writings,* vol. XI, p. 119.

73. ". . : it is not likely that such a scheme as this could have been set on foot in France, and that Deane could have been consulted about it, and acquiesced in the proposal, without at least the knowledge if not the secret connivance of the French government." Stillé, *Comte de Broglie,* etc., pp. 372-73.

74. His correspondence was filed under the *F* in Washington's letter-book. Fitzpatrick, *George Washington Himself,* p. 308.

75. "I was never made acquainted with a single circumstance relating to it." *Writings,* vol. XI, p. 158. In a private letter to Thomas Nelson, Jr., February 8 (vol. X, p. 433), he refers to the Canadian expedition as a "child of folly," and disclaims any connection with it.

76. Baurmeister, p. 163.

77. It is only fair to Rush to point out that he obviously did think of Gates as a genius, as witness also his letter to John Adams, October 4, just after Germantown. Goodman, *Benjamin Rush,* pp. 112-13. See Appendix I, volume II, of the Butterfield edition of Rush's *Letters* for an excellent discussion of this.

78. Compare with Beveridge, *John Marshall,* vol. I, p. 121: "Gates was its figurehead, Conway its brain, Wilkinson its tool, Rush its amanuenesis, and certain members of Congress its accessories before the fact."

79. Hatch, *Administration,* p. 78.

80. Most shrilly by Charles Francis Adams in *Studies Military and Diplomatic.* Here was the grandson of that John Adams who found so much fault with Washington *during* the Revolution.

81. Of two famous parents-of-the-future, Zebulon Pike, Sr., who was to sire the peak-discoverer, was a captain in Moylan's, but Light-Horse Harry Lee, father of Robert E. Lee, had not yet joined the Continental army.

82. This may remain a mystery. The red coat, surely the most famous garment in modern military history, was introduced into the New Model Army of 1644-45. That shade of scarlet is of course the British royal color; but British royal colors, like British royal everything else, were not popular in England at the time, the Puritans preferring grays and browns, even black; nor was scarlet the color of Cromwell's personal bodyguard, which was green-and-silver. Fortescue, "A Chapter on Red Coats," pp. 385-89.

83. Freeman, vols. I, II, III, and IV, *passim;* also Marx, "Medical Profile."

84. Palmer, *Steuben,* p. 2.

85. Palmer gives no authority. Nor is there any reference to this little white lie, the sort of thing that Franklin loved, anywhere in Franklin's voluminous correspondence. It is not difficult to think that Franklin would have concocted such a scheme, but it is hard to believe that he would have resisted the temptation to chat about it later, when the revelation could do no harm.

86. Sometimes he implied that it was Swabia, sometimes Baden. Neither place had ever authorized the rank of lieutenant general. Palmer, *Steuben,* p. 138 n.

87. Ward, vol. II, p. 554; Palmer, p. 157.

88. Laurens, *Correspondence,* p. 126.

89. Kapp, *Steuben,* pp. 114-28.

90. Curtis, *Organization of the British Army,* p. 15.

91. "Their very hats and swords weighed very near as much as the whole equipment of one of our soldiers. The worst British regiment in the service would with ease have marched two miles for their one." Stedman, vol. I, p. 331.

92. Though put to use right away, even as it was being written, it was not published in book form until the following year, 1779, in Philadelphia. Kapp, *Steuben,* chap. X.

93. He stayed here after the war, died here, and is buried near a town named after him, Steubenville, N.Y., the site being now a state park. Ben Walker was one of his pallbearers.

94. Gardiner, *Varnum,* pp. 188-89.

95. The blossoms the boys at Valley Forge that spring saw —and they must have seen them, whichever way they looked— were all white. The pink blossoms that form so sensational a feature of the scene at Valley Forge Park today are a later development, a cultivation.

96. The best description of this famous do is André's own, as contained in the Lodge-edited *Journal.* See also Sargent, *Major John André,* pp. 167-77.

Appendix One

TODAY Valley Forge is a place of beauty. Butterflies flutter there, and under oak trees picnickers line the rustic picnic tables, making the groves loud with laughter. There are roadways and shaded walks, and lovely rolling lawns, and in the spring people come from hundreds of miles around to see this park's greatest glory—the dogwoods in bloom.

There are two museums in the two thousand and odd acres of woodland and landscaped parkland. There is a huge memorial arch. There are many log huts built in company streets as they had been built in 1777. There is a chapel, a carillon tower, an observatory on the top of Mount Joy. Colonel Dewee's house—called the Bake House because of the ovens that still may be seen in its cellar—holds the library and the office of the park commission, a place of business now as it was that terrible winter: it was here that most of the officers took the oath of allegiance, here that the courts martial were held. The Deborah Hewes house has been furnished with period furniture, and a replica of the Commander in Chief's blue flag (the original is in one of the museums) flies from a staff. There are of course many monuments and markers, statues and such. There are "Keep Off the Grass" signs, and —what would have startled the soldiers even more—signs that read: "Keep Off the Entrenchments."

It was not always thus. For a hundred years after the Continentals had marched away that hillside was a neglected tangle of underbrush and rotting tree stumps. It was not until the centenary celebration of June 19, 1878, that action was started, by private patriotic interests, to buy the headquarters building. The memorial association, however, had hard going of it, financially; and not until May 30, 1893, when the State of Pennsylvania took over, did the park begin to take its present form. The rebuilding of the huts, the blacksmithy, the artillery park, the hospital, and all the rest, followed.

Though the government at Washington did put up the memorial arch that dominates the landscape, Valley Forge is and presumably will continue to be not a national park, as so many visitors appear to believe, but a state park.

High on that memorial arch are engraved the words written of the Continental soldiers at Valley Forge by the man who perhaps knew them best of all, their Commander in Chief:

"Naked and starving as they are we cannot enough admire the incomparable patience and fidelity of the soldiery."

Another quotation that the visitor would do well to read—though it is not engraved on any monument—is this, from the oration of Henry Armitt Brown at the exercises marking the hundredth anniversary of the evacuation of Valley Forge:

"If heroic deeds can consecrate a spot of earth, if the living be still sensible of the example of the dead, if courage be yet a common virtue and patience in suffering be still honorable, in your sight, if freedom be any longer precious and faith in humanity be not banished from among you, if love of country still finds a refuge among the hearts of men, 'take your shoes from off your feet, for the place on which you stand is holy ground.' "

Appendix Two

THE FOLLOWING, taken from the *Journals of the Continental Congress,* vol. VII, pp. 355-59, is the quartermaster general's department report, adopted May 14, 1777—the law, that is, under which supplies were raised and moved, when they were, at the time of the Valley Forge winter:

1. That the quarter master general of the army be authorized and empowered to appoint one commissary of forage for the army, and one for each of the military departments thereof, with such and so many forage masters as he shall judge necessary.

2. That the duty of the commissary of forage shall be to purchase such quantities of forage, and store the same in such magazines as the quarter master general, or the deputy quarter master general, of any department, shall, from time to time, order and direct. That the commissaries shall conform themselves in making purchases to such rules and regulations as

shall be prescribed to them by the quarter master general, or deputy quarter master general of the department to which they shall severally belong.

3. That all forage purchased by any commissary of forage, and delivered into any magazine, shall be received by the forage master thereunto appointed, who shall give his receipts therefor, specifying the sort, quantity, and quality, as a voucher for the commissary of forage, to be by him produced to the quarter master general or deputy quarter master general of the department in support of his account.

4. That the commissaries of forage shall make a monthly return to the quarter master general or deputy quarter master general of the department, of all forage by them purchased, specifying to what forage master, and into which magazine the same was delivered, that the forage master may stand charged therewith.

5. That no forage master, to whose care any magazine of forage shall be committed, shall issue any part thereof unless by a written order of the commander in chief, the commander in chief of the department, the commanding officer of the post where such a magazine may be established, the quarter master general or deputy quarter master general of the department, or one of his assistants, the waggon master general, or any other waggon master; such orders to specify for whose use the forage is intended; and every such order to be filed by the forage master, and a regular entry thereof made in a book to be by him kept for that purpose, as a voucher for the expenditure of the forage by him received.

6. That the forage master shall make monthly returns to the quarter master general and deputy quarter master general of the departments they belong to, of the state of their magazines, specifying the quantity left in store at the first and every succeeding return, the quantity received since the last return, the expenditure since such return, and what remains on hand.

7. And whereas it frequently happens that there is a necessity to detain hired carriages, the owners whereof were to find their own forage, far beyond the time for which the owners thereof

agreed to serve, and who, if their own forage is expended, must have recourse to the public magazines, it is resolved, that such persons so detained and become destitute of forage, shall, upon the written order of any of the officers mentioned in the fifth resolution, be supplied out of the public magazines; and that the waggon master, before he signs the discharge for any such hired carriage, shall direct the forage master to endorse thereon the quantity, sort and quality of the forage furnished such person, that the same may be deducted out of the wages due to the owner of such hired carriage; all of which deductions shall, by the quarter master general or deputy quarter master of the department, be carried to the credit of the forage masters' account, who shall have furnished the forage.

8. That if the commissary of forage in any department should be ordered to procure such large quantities of forage as to render it impossible for him to do it without assistance, the quarter master general or deputy quarter master general of the department shall direct one or more of his assistants to aid the commissary of forage, pointing out the districts in which they are severally to purchase, that one may not enhance the price by bidding above another.

9. Whereas, notwithstanding the orders that have been from time to time issued by general officers of our army, to prevent the loss and embezzlement of intrenching tools, and other military stores, great waste hath been made; to prevent which, for the future, it is resolved, that every commissary of stores, store keeper, or person to whose charge and care any military stores of what kind soever shall be committed, shall pass his receipt for, and stand charged to be accountable for the same, and shall not issue any of them without taking a receipt therefor, the receiver promising to be accountable: and if any person having received any such stores, shall lose or embezzle the same, the commissary, store keeper, or person by whom they were delivered, shall charge him with the value thereof, and transmit a copy of such charge to the pay master general or deputy pay master general of the department, who is to charge the same to the pay master of the corps such person may belong

to, unless it shall appear that such loss happened without any blameable negligence or omission; and if any person in the continental service shall sell or otherwise dispose of any stores committed to his care, without a written order for so doing, issued by the commander in chief or commander in chief of the department, or by a general officer commanding at a separate post, he shall be punished for theft.

10. That the waggon master general of the army, or waggon master in any of the departments thereof, shall receive from the quarter master general or deputy quarter master general of any department, all such horses, cattle, and carriages as the service may require; and that neither the waggon master general, or any other waggon master shall, on any account, presume to purchase any horses, cattle, or carriages for the public service, without the express order of the commander in chief, the commander in chief of the department, the quarter master general or deputy quarter master general of a department; nor shall the waggon master general, or any other waggon master, hire any horses, cattle or carriages, unless by the authority aforesaid, or by that of an assistant deputy quarter master general.

11. That the quarter master general appoint such assistants and make such arrangements for conducting the business of his department, as to him and to the commander in chief, and commander of the departments, shall seem most conducive to the public weal; that a copy of such arrangement, specifying the names of the assistants, commissaries of forage, waggon master, forage masters, and clerks of the several departments, to be transmitted to the Board of War: and that every assistant of the quarter master general of the army, and every assistant of the deputy quarter master general of the several departments thereof, shall make monthly returns of every article, of what kinds soever, that may be in or at any of the forts, encampments, magazines, or places in the district, committed to his care, to the deputy quarter master general of the department, noting what is good, what is reparable, and what it unfit for further service, in separate columns; from which returns, the

deputy quarter master general shall make one general return, in which shall be specified the total of all the articles in every district within his department; one copy thereof shall be monthly transmitted to the Board of War, one to the commander in chief of the department, and one to the quarter master general; from which returns, the quarter master general shall make a general return, specifying what is in each department and every district thereof; one copy whereof shall be monthly transmitted to the Board of War, one to the commander in chief, and one to the commander of each department.

12. That every assistant quarter master, commissary of forage, waggon master general, forage master, and every other person employed in the quarter master general's branch, who shall neglect or refuse to make such monthly returns, shall be dismissed from the service by the quarter master general or the deputy quarter master general of the department to which the delinquent belongs.

13. And in order that all deputy quarter masters general and assistants may make their returns in such a manner as to avoid that great confusion which has heretofor arisen from a want of method, the quarter master general is to furnish his deputies with a form, copies whereof they are to deliver to the assistants and to every person in the quarter master general's branch who may be called upon for a return.

14. That the quarter master general and the deputy quarter masters general in the several departments, have full power and be authorized, with the consent of the commander in chief, or the commander of the department, to dismiss any person by them employed, who shall refuse or neglect any duty enjoined by the foregoing resolutions, or any other duty he may be charged with, and to appoint others in the stead of such as may be dismissed.

15. The general and commander in chief of our armies, and the commander of any department thereof, shall be allowed as much forage for their horses and those of their suite as the service may require.

16. That a major general and brigadier general, not having the command of a separate department, shall each be allowed forage for six horses for themselves, their aids-de-camp, or brigade majors and servants.

17. That the commander in chief, and the commander in any separate department, be authorized to allow such quantities of forage, and for and during such times as they shall think proper, to the quarter master general and his deputies, to the muster master general and his deputies, the chief engineer and his assistants, the commissary general and his assistants, the director general of the hospital, his subs and surgeons general, to the adjutant general and his deputies, to the colonels, lieutenant colonels, majors, adjutants, quarter masters, and surgeons of regiments, and to provost marshals, or to such and so many of the before mentioned officers and their deputies as the service shall necessarily require; Provided, always, that if any of the officers abovementioned, their deputies or assistants, should be allowed forage in consequence of any general orders hereafter given, and should nevertheless not keep any or so many horses as they would be permitted to draw forage for, that in such case, no forage shall be issued for more horses than they really have, nor shall they at any time thereafter be allowed any forage as back allowance or any money in lieu thereof.

18. That a deputy quarter master general be appointed to each department, and one to each grand division of the army; the rank of the former to be that of a colonel, of the latter, that of a lieutenant colonel.

19. That the quarter master general, with the approbation of the commander in chief, or commander in any separate department, appoint a competent number of deputy quarter masters general, a waggon master general, and so many waggon masters, as the service, from time to time, may require, and to make a return to the Board of War, of the names of the persons so appointed.

20. That Major General Mifflin be allowed, for his services

as quarter master general, 166 dollars per month, in addition to his pay as major general.

That the pay of a deputy quarter master general of a grand division of the army, be seventy-five dollars per month.

That the pay of an assistant deputy quarter master general be forty dollars per month, and that he have the rank of a captain:

That the pay of a waggon master general be seventy-five dollars per month,

That the pay of a deputy waggon master general be fifty dollars per month,

That the pay of a barrack master general be seventy-five dollars per month,

That the pay of a waggon master or conductor of waggons be forty dollars per month:

That the pay of a forage master be forty dollars per month.

Appendix Three

ON JUNE 10, 1777, Joseph Trumbull having announced his intention of resigning, Congress, perhaps in part to make up for the brevity of its quartermaster general's report, adopted *in toto* the following resolution:

I. That for supplying the army of the United States with provisions, one commissary general and four deputy commissaries general of purchases, and one commissary general and three deputy commissaries general of issues, be appointed by Congress.

II. That each of the said commissaries and deputy commissaries be authorized to appoint for himself one clerk.

III. That the deputy commissaries general have authority to appoint as many assistant commissaries to act under them as may from time to time be necessary, and the same to displace at pleasure, making returns thereof to the commissaries general respectively, who shall have full power to limit their numbers, to displace such as they shall think disqualified for the trust, and direct their respective deputy commissaries general to appoint others in their stead: that special care be taken by the several officers empowered as aforesaid, to appoint none but persons of probity, capacity, vigilance, and attachment to the United States, and the cause they are engaged in; and to make returns to the Board of War, the commander in chief, and the commander of the respective departments, of the assistant commissaries by them respectively appointed, their several places of abode, the time of their appointment and commission, and the post, place, magazine or district to which they are severally assigned; and that the deputy commissaries general of purchases and issues in the same district make similar returns to each other.

IV. That the commissary general of purchases shall superintend the deputy commissaries general of purchases, and assign to each a separate district, who shall constantly reside therein, and not make any purchases beyond the limits thereof; and that every purchaser employed therein shall also have a certain district assigned to him by the respective deputy commissary general, in which he shall reside, and beyond the limits of which he shall not be permitted to make any purchases, unless by special order of his superior, directing the quantity and quality of provisions so to be purchased beyond his limits, and informing such purchaser of the prices given by the stationed purchaser in the district to which he may be sent.

V. That the commissary general of purchases shall direct the deputy commissaries general in their respective districts, to inform themselves and assistants, as nearly as may be, of the prices for which the articles, which they are to procure, may be purchased, and that neither they nor any of the said assistants under their direction, exceed such prices; and if any deputy commissary general of purchases shall neglect his duty, or be guilty of any fraud or misconduct in his office, the commissary general may suspend him, and shall immediately certify the same to Congress, with the reasons for such suspension, and appoint a person to act in his stead, with all the powers of a deputy commissary general, until the sense of Congress shall be known thereon.

VI. That the present commissary general, by himself or his deputies, deliver unto the commissary general of issues, or his deputies or assistants, all and every kind of provisions and other public stores in the commissary's department, that now are, or at the time when such delivery shall be made, may be, in any of the forts, places, magazines and store houses belonging to the United States, taking duplicate receipts for the same, one set whereof, together with a general return of all stores so delivered, to be sent to the Board of Treasury, that the commissary general of issues may be charged therewith.

VII. That it shall be the duty of the commissary general of purchases, with the assistance of the deputy commissaries general and assistant commissaries of purchases, to purchase all provisions and other necessaries allowed, or which may hereafter be allowed by Congress to the troops of the United States, and deliver the same to the commissary general of issues, or his deputies or assistants, in such qualities, and at such places or magazines as the commander in chief, or the commander of the respective department shall direct.

VIII. That the commissary general of issues shall direct the respective deputy commissaries general, to station one of their assistants at every fort, post, place or magazine where provisions are or may be stored.

IX. That the commissary of purchases shall furnish each of the deputy commissaries general and assistants, with a book, in which is to be entered every purchase by them respectively made: that all the accounts may be kept in the same form, he shall cause the pages of such books to be divided into ten columns, in the first of which shall be entered the year, month and day in which any purchase is made; in the second, the name of the person from whom; in the third, in what place; in the fourth, the species and quantity of provisions, and if live stock, the number, colour and natural marks; in the fifth, the artificial marks and number; in the sixth, the prices; in the seventh, the amount of the purchase money; in the eighth, ninth and tenth, the weight of the meat, hides and tallow of the live stock as hereinafter directed: and the commissary general of issues shall furnish each of the issuing commissaries general and assistants with a similar book, in which shall be entered all provisions received by them from the purchasers respectively, the first column to contain the time of receiving such provisions; the second, the name of the purchaser; and in each of the other columns, the entries before directed.

X. That each purchaser shall enter, in distinct pages of the said book, each species of provisions by him purchased, and, at the end of every month, shall foot and transfer the said entries to a general account, specifying the quantity, amount, and average cost of each article, and shall also, in the course of the next succeeding month, send a copy of such account to the respective deputy commissary generals, who shall thereupon make out a monthly return of all the provisions purchased in his district, specifying the quantity, amount, and average cost of each species, as before directed, together with a copy of each purchaser's account, to the Board of War and commissary general of purchases, within the time limited as aforesaid. And whereas it is necessary that separate and distinct accounts should be kept of every species of provision purchased that as many sheets shall be ruled into Columns as above directed as there are articles to be purchased in one of which all purchases of Flour shall be entered in another all purchases of Salted Meat in distinct Columns. Each of these to be footed at the end of every Month and transfered to one General Account and every purchaser shall also in the Course of the next succeeding Month send a Copy of the General Account to the respective D. Com General of purchases of the Department in which such purchases were made, and that the Accounts of every Deputy Commissary General of purchases may be kept in the same Form, they are each to open a Book in which is to be entered, under the different Heads of Flour, salted Meat, &c the Amount of each Species drawn from every purchasers Account Current with the Amount thereof, the purchasers Name and the averaged Price. Each of these to be footed at the End of every Month, and the Average of the Agregate drawn and then transferred to one General account, Copies of each of which shall be sent by the Deputy Commissary General of purchases made up to the first Day of the Month in which such Accounts were directed to be sent by the preceding Rtaicle to the Board of War and one other Copy to the Commissary General of purchases. That the Commissary General of purchases shall deliver all provisions by him or his Deputies purchased into the Magazine within, or into that nearest to, the District in which the purchases are made, unless otherwise directed by the Commissary General of Issues or his D. Commissary General in any Department and unless it be live Stock, which is always to be sent to such places as the Commissary General of Issues or his D. Commissary General in any Department shall direct. That whatever provisions or Stores may be sent to any post place or Magazine by any purchaser shall be accompanied by Duplicate Invoices, taken from the Entries directed to be made in the Books mentioned in the 10th and 12th Articles, one of which together with the provisions or Stores shall be delivered by the stationed Commissary of purchases there to the issuing Commissary for his Use, who on the other shall give his Receipt for so much thereof as he may receive which receipt shall be transmitted by the sd stationed Commissary to the purchaser.

XI. That the purchasing commissaries deliver live stock and other provisions required by the commissary, or several deputy commissaries general of issues, at such places as they shall respectively direct.

XII. That the deputy commissary general of purchases in each district shall specially appoint one or more assistants to purchase live stock, who shall cause to be branded on the horns of all cattle by them purchased, the number and initial letters of their names respectively; and shall also have power to employ drovers, and a person of each place, to which they may respectively be directed to send cattle, to receive, kill, and deliver the same, as hereafter directed. That every Creature purchased for the Use of the Army shall immediately thereafter be branded with the initial Letters of the purchasing Commissary's Name and the first Creature purchased by such Commissary shall be branded on the Horns with the Figure 1, the second with the Figure 2 and so on.

XIII. That each drove of live stock, or quantity of provisions or other stores, that may be sent to any post, place, or magazine, by any purchaser, shall be accompanied with duplicate invoices, taken from the entries directed to be made in the books of the purchasing commissaries, one of which, together with the live stock or other stores, shall be delivered at such post, place, or magazine, to the person appointed to receive live stock, or to the issuing commissaries respectively, who, on the other hand, shall give his receipt for the articles received, to be transmitted to the purchaser by the person delivering the said articles; provided, that, if any live stock, under the care of the drover, shall be wanted at any other post than that to which they were ordered, the purchaser's deputy at such post may detain them, taking a copy of the invoice, as far as it respects the live stock detained, and giving his receipt for the same on the back of the said invoice, specifying their marks and numbers, and the person to whom the residue may be delivered, shall give his receipt therefor on the same invoice, and detain the other for his use as aforesaid.

XIV. That each drove of live stock shall be killed under the direction of the purchaser's deputy receiving the same, who shall weigh and deliver the meat to the commissary of issues of the respective posts, together with duplicates of the invoice left by the drover, entering in the eighth column the weight of the quarters of the several creatures; in the ninth, the weight of the hides; in the tenth, the weight of the tallow; and at the foot of each invoice, the number of heads and tongues; and the commissary of issues shall endorse his receipt on one of the invoices, and deliver it to the deputy aforesaid, who shall return it to the purchaser as his voucher, and to enable him to fill up the eighth, ninth, and tenth columns of the entries in his book; and the other shall be kept by the issuing commissary for his own use. That the Commissary General of purchases specially appoint Deputy Commissaries in each Department to purchase Live Stock, giving power to the said purchasers so appointed to employ persons at such post as the Commissary or Deputy Commissary General shall direct, to receive and kill the Cattle and to deliver the Meat, Hide, Tallow, Head and Tongues to the Commissary of Issues at such post.

XV. That the commissary general of purchases shall contract, by himself, or the respective deputy commissaries general, with one or more persons in each district, to make or supply a sufficient quantity of vinegar for the use of the army.

XVI. That the deputy commissaries of purchases take special care to procure full supplies of vegetables, as being essentially necessary to the health of the army; and they are respectively empowered and directed, with the advice of the commander in chief, or commander of the respective district, to hire land therein, and raise such quantities of vegetables as are wanted, and cannot be otherwise procured for the army; and for this purpose, to employ suitable persons to conduct, and labourers to assist in carrying on the said business. And whereas Experience has evinced that potatoes can be preserved in such a Manner as that the Crops of one Year will keep until that of the succeeding Year is fit for Use; the Com. General or the D. Com. Generals in each Department by and with the Advice of the Commander in Chief or Commander of the Department shall therefore fix upon one or more proper places in each Department on which to raise such Quantities of potatoes, Turnips and other Vegetables as the Commander in Chief or Commander of a Department may direct, to rent Land therefor and employ persons to superintend and carry on the Works with a sufficient Number of Labourers.

XVII. That the commissary general of purchases shall, from time to time, apply to Congress for all the money wanted in his department, and shall make the necessary advances to the respective deputy commissaries general, calling them to account as often as he shall judge it necessary; and the deputy commissaries general shall, in like manner, make advances of the money received of the said commissary general to their respective assistants, and call them to account as aforesaid.

XVIII. That the commissary and deputy commissaries general of purchases and issues, shall respectively be accountable for the conduct of the officers of their own appointment, and all the accounts of purchases and issues shall, once in six months, be settled by the respective commissaries general with the proper commissioners of accounts; each account of purchases to be vouched by the several bills and receipts of the venders, specifying the cost, and the receipts of the issuing commissaries, shewing the delivery of all articles therein charged; and each account of issue by the original victualling returns hereafter directed to be made, and receipts for all provisions charged therein as rations, or sent by the respective issuing commissary to any other; and the commissaries general shall produce the monthly returns of the several purchasing and issuing commissaries, to be used by the commissioners in adjusting the respective accounts.

XIX. That the commissaries general of purchases and issues, and their respective deputies, for neglect of duty, or other offences in their respective offices, shall be subject to military arrest and trial, by order of the commander in chief, or any general officer commanding a division of the army, post, or department, where such neglect of duty or offence may happen; and the respective assistants of the deputy commissaries general of purchases and issues, shall, for the same causes, be liable to military arrest as commissioned officers in the army, by any general officer, or any officer commanding at a detached post to which such assistants may be assigned.

XX. That the commissary general of issues shall superintend the respective deputy commissaries general, and assign to each a separate district, as already provided for the commissary general of purchases.

XXI. That every issuing commissary shall enter, in distinct pages of the book mentioned in the ninth article, each species of provisions or other stores received by him, including the provisions delivered by other issuing commissaries, or the present commissary general, and the same entries shall be made with respect to these, as therein are directed, when provisions are received from the purchasers; excepting that the prices and cost of articles, delivered by the said commissaries, may be omitted.

XXII. That every issuing commissary shall be furnished with a book of issues, in which he shall open a separate account with each regiment, corps, or detachment to which he may issue, or commissary to which he may send or deliver provisions; and each page thereof shall be divided into columns, in the first of which shall be entered the time of delivery; in the second, the name of the officer upon whose return provisions are issued, or by whom sent to any other issuing commissary; in the third, the number of rations, and, in other separate columns, the several quantities of each species of provisions delivered as rations, or sent to the commissaries as aforesaid. And, on the last day of every month, he shall foot the said accounts, and also all the accounts of provisions received and entered in the book mentioned in the preceding article.

XXIII. That every issuing commissary shall take duplicate receipts for each quantity of provisions and stores by him sent to any post, place or magazine, agreeable to the form of the entries directed to be made in the book of issues, one of which he shall deliver to the officer, or person employed to deliver the said provisions or stores, and the issuing commissary at such post, place, or magazine, or at any intermediate post, who may receive such provisions or stores, or any part thereof, shall certify the quality on the back of the said receipt, which the officer, or person who delivered the provisions, shall return to the commissary that sent them as his voucher: And, in cases of deficiency, the commissary who sent the provisions shall credit the commissary to whom they were directed for the quantity lost, if the same has been placed to his debit, and shall charge twice the amount thereof to the account of the officer or person employed to deliver it, and shall also transmit a copy of the said account to the pay master or deputy pay master general in the district, who shall send to the issuing commissary a receipt for such account, to be produced by him on settlement, and shall also deduct the amount thereof from the pay of the delinquent, and credit the United States therefor: provided, that if any provisions or stores shall be lost by unavoidable accident, and the same is proved by sworn evidence before the commanding officer of the post from or to which such provisions or stores were sent, his certificate, with the proof annexed, shall authorize the commissary to cancel such charge. The D Commissary General of Issues and his Deputies to take Duplicate Receipts of all provisions and Stores of what Kind soever by them forwarded from one post, place or Magazine to another specifying every Specie sent, its Condition; the Time when: the person or persons by whom, delivering at the same Time one of the Receipts to the person taking the provision or Stores in Charge. Upon the delivery thereof to the Commissary to whom they were directed, or other intermediate Commissary of Issues such Commissary to endorse on the Back of the Receipt a Certificate acknowledging the Receipt, or such part thereof as may be delivered, but if there shall be a Deficiency in any of the Articles, the Commissary who was to have received the same or to whom the residue may be delivered shall mark the Deficiency on the Back of the Receipt; give Credit for the whole of what was sent, and charge the public with the Deficiency and transmit a Monthly Return to the Commissary General of Issues, or Deputy Com. General of the Department; who shall from all the Returns make out one general Account of such Deficiencies, if any, and transmit the same to the pay Master General or D pay Master General of the Department that he may, and he is hereby required, to charge the same to the Account of the pay Master of the Regiment to which such delinquents respectively may belong who are to deduct the Amount out of the Delinquents pay. Provided always that if any provisions or Stores shall be lost by unavoidable accidents and the same can be proved to be so, by sworn Witnesses before any officer commanding at the post from which provisions of Stores were sent, such officer's Certificate with the proofs annexed shall be a sufficient Voucher to the Commissary to cancel such Charge made against the person or Persons losing the same.

XXIV. That no provisions be issued to any persons but by the written order of the commander in chief, the commander of any department, the quarter master general, any of his deputies or assistants, the commanding officer of a post, describing the persons in whose favour such order shall be given; or upon a return signed by the commanding officer of a corps, or detachment thereof, whether commissioned or non-commissioned, or by the regimental quarter master.

XXV. That when any troops are ordered to quit a post, and the issuing commissary remains at such post, the respective commanding officers of such regiment or corps shall call upon the issuing commissary for a certificate, specifying the day to which they were victualled, inclusively; and, in case detachments of different regiments or corps are made, the commanding officer of such detachments shall procure a certificate from the commissary, in which shall be inserted the days to which the different troops, of which his detachment may be composed, were victualled, and the next, and every subsequent provision return for such detachment shall distinguish the corps out of which it is formed, and the number of each corps, to the end that the commissary may charge each corps with the provision issued to it; and if any commissary, at any other post, shall victual any corps or detachment comprehended in the foregoing description before such certificates are produced, he shall charge the officer commanding the same, with twenty days' provision for the whole number of men under his care, and make return thereof to the pay master general or deputy pay master general in the district, who shall make the proper stoppages, and also to the board of treasury, who shall charge him therefor. Provided, That if such certificate be procured and delivered within thirty days after the drawing of such provisions without certificate, the commissary general shall cancel the charge, keeping the certificate as a voucher for so doing: Provided also,

That notwithstanding such certificate may be produced, if it shall appear that the officer commanding any corps or detachment, has drawn more provisions than the corps or detachment was entitled to, he shall stand charged the double quantity so over-drawn.

XXVI. That every issuing commissary shall take receipts for the number of rations, and for so much of every species of provisions as he may issue therefor.

XXVII. That every issuing commissary, on the last drawing day preceding the last day of every month, shall victual the troops up to the last day of the month inclusive; and if provisions should be ordered for troops going on detachments, for such time as would run beyond that day, two returns shall be made out, one to the last day of the month inclusive, and one from the first day of the month inclusive to the time ordered.

XXVIII. That every issuing commissary shall number the provision returns, and endorse the same with the date thereof, and the number of men victualled, and put the returns of each detachment or corps in separate files, each to contain the returns of a month for such corps or detachments.

XXIX. That, wherever any capital magazine shall be established, the commander in chief, or commanding officer of the department, shall order store-houses to be built, and a barrack for fifty men, and the same to be enclosed with a stockade.

XXX. That, whenever any of the provisions or stores in any of the magazines become so damaged as to threaten a total loss of such damaged provisions, the commissary of issues, to whose care such provisions may be committed, shall make return thereof immediately to the deputy commissary general of issues, who is to apply to the commander in chief, or some general officer, to order a court of enquiry, who shall thereupon grant one, and such provisions as may by the court be condemned, shall be sold at public vendue, under the direction of the deputy commissary of issues, public notice being given of such sale, by advertisements at least ten days before the day of sale, unless the court should determine that the same ought to be sold at an earlier day.

XXXI. That every assistant commissary of issue shall, within six days after the last day of every month, make a return to the deputy commissary general of the district, of all provisions and stores in his magazine or store, at the last preceding return; of all provisions by him received in the preceding month; from whom and whence; of what he has forwarded, to whom and to what place; of what he has issued, specifying the regiment and corps, and the number of rations, and quantity of each species of provisions drawn by the same; and of what remains in store.

XXXII. That each deputy commissary of issue shall, from the monthly returns of the assistant commissaries, make out a general return for the district, specifying what remained in the magazines or stores at the last return; what has been received since; the number of rations and quantity of provisions issued, and what remains in store, distinguishing the several posts, places, magazines, and regiments or corps as aforesaid; one to be sent to the Board of War, one to the commander in chief, one to the commander of the department, one to the commissary general of purchases, and one to the commissary general of issues.

XXXIII. That the commissary general of purchases and commissary general of issues, each in his own department, make a general monthly return to the Board of War, the commander in chief, and the commanding officer of the respective districts, and take special care constantly to provide and furnish each of the officers under him with printed forms of the books, invoices, receipts, and returns, to be used by them respectively, agreeable to these resolves.

XXXIV. That no returns of rations drawn or returned by the several regiments be hereafter made by the issuing commissaries to the commissary general of musters, or by him to the adjutant general, or by the adjutant general to the Board of War, as directed in the regulations of the muster master's department, passed by Congress the 4th of April last.

XXXV. That the commissaries general and the respective officers under them, apply to the quarter master general, or his respective officers, for waggons, teams, and horses, wanted in the several districts; and if, at any time, it shall be necessary to hire the same, they are not to exceed the rates stipulated by Congress, or the quarter master general aforesaid.

XXXVI. That all persons employed to purchase for the United States any articles in the several departments of the commissary general of provisions, quarter master, director, or clothier general, or the commissary general of military stores, shall previously apply to them, or the principal officers under them respectively, for certificates of the several prices by them allowed for such articles, and shall not, on any pretence whatever, exceed such prices. And it is recommended to the several States to give their purchasers respectively similar directions.

XXXVII. That the commissary general of purchases from time to time provide sufficient quantities of salt, and deliver it to the commissary general of issues, or the respective officers under him, who are directed to issue to the troops only such quantities, and in such manner, as the commander in chief, or commander of the respective district, shall direct. And the commissary general of issues shall direct the respective deputy commissaries general to employ a suitable number of coopers, who shall salt and pack provisions at the several magazines and stores, and take the proper precautions with respect to all provisions therein deposited.

XXXVIII. And whereas, great confusion has arisen from the manner in which officers and soldiers have been paid for rations and parts of rations allowed to, but not drawn by, them respectively, *Resolved,* That the parts of a ration be estimated as follows, viz: for the daily allowance of beef, pork, or fish, 4-90ths of a dollar; of bread or flower, 2-90ths; of peas or beans, 1-90th; of milk, 1-90th; of beer, 1-90th; of rice, 1-180th; and of soap, 1-180th; making 10-90ths of a dollar for each ration; and that, for the future, the quarter master, or person drawing provision for any regiment, corps, or detachment, and delivering the same to the respective issuing commissary, who shall compare it with his books, and finding it right, shall certify thereon that the several charges in the abstract are just, and that such a sum as he shall find to be due, should be paid to the respective pay master of the regiment, corps, or detachment, who shall annex the said abstract to the pay roll, that the pay master, or deputy pay master general of the district, may, and he is hereby required to pay, such ration abstract to the regimental pay master, who is directed to pay the respective officers and soldiers, and take their receipts. And when any regiment, corps, or detachment, or issuing commissary is ordered to leave a post before the end of the month, the ration abstracts shall be made up to the day of his or their leaving the post, and certified by the Commissary as aforesaid. Whereas great Confusion hath arisen from the manner in which officers rations are drawn or paid for to prevent which in future Every provision return for any Corps or detachment shall Include the officers for as many days as the return is made out for and at the rate of one Ration per day and Every such return shall specify the Number of officers, and their rank as well as that of the Non-Com: Officers and privates for which provision is to be drawn, and In order that the Officers may be regularly paid for the residue of the Rations allowed them. The paymaster of each regiment or Corps shall make a monthly Abstract of the Number of rations due to the Officers of the Corps they severally belong to and Charge the same in the Accounts Current with the paymaster General or deputy Paymaster General of the several departments who are hereby required to allow the same. Whereas it frequently happens that the Troops cannot be supplied with every Specie of provisions allowed by Congress and a difference of Opinion of what is a real Equivalent has arisen, to avoid which in future, that 2 lb of Beef shall be equal to one Ration of all species, or 1½ lb of pork or 3½ lb. Flour or 6½ pints of peas or Beans or 7 pints of Milk or 10 pints of Indian Meal or 5 pints of Rice or 1¼ pints of Molasses, or 1½ lb hard Soap or 1½ lb. soft Soap.

XXXIX. That the commissary of issues at every post where cattle are killed for the use of the army, appoint a careful person to take charge of the hides and tallow, to see that the former are properly dried, and that the latter is properly rendered, and that both are disposed of as the commissary general of issues, by order of Congress, shall direct.

XL. That the commissary and deputy commissaries general of purchases in each department, and every purchaser employed under them, shall take the oath of fidelity to the United States, and the following oath or affirmation, viz.

I ______, do solemnly and sincerely swear or affirm in the presence of Almighty God, that I will not collude with any person or persons whatever to enhance the price of provisions, or any article of commerce which I shall at any time hereafter be directed to purchase for the use of the United States; and that I will endeavor, by every honest means in my power, to procure the articles which I may be directed to purchase at the most reasonable rates; and that I will not charge the public with any advance on any purchases by me to be made, and that I will, in all things, conduct myself as becometh a faithful servant of the public.

XLI. That the commissary and the deputy commissary general of issues in each department, and every issuing commissary employed under them, shall take the said oath of fidelity, and the following oath or affirmation, viz.

I do swear or affirm that I will faithfully receive, take care of, and issue the provisions and other stores committed to my trust, and keep regular accounts and make regular returns, agreeable to the resolutions of Congress, and oftener if thereupon required by any superior officer having right to order returns; and that I will, in all things, honestly demean myself as a faithful servant of the public.

Appendix Four

Moved by the complaints of those who had to work the complicated machinery of the commissariat, Congress, October 4, 1777, made certain amendments, as follows:

1. *Resolved,* That if the deputy commissary general of purchases, or of issues, appointed for the eastern district, shall decline to accept of, or officiate in, their respective offices, Major General Putnam, the commanding officer at Peekskill, or the commanding officer there for the time being, be authorized and directed to appoint suitable persons to those respective offices, or either of them; and that Major General Gates, or the commanding officer for the time being of the northern department, have similar power with respect to the deputy commissary general of purchases and of issues for the northern department, and that they respectively certify the names of the commissaries, which they may appoint, to Congress, for their approbation.

2. *Resolved,* That every assistant appointed, or that hereafter may be appointed by the respective deputy commissaries general of purchases and of issues, shall enter into bond to the president of Congress, in the penalty of 5,000 dollars, for the faithful performance of his duty; and such bond, being taken by the deputy commissary general, and lodged with the pay master general, or deputy pay master general of the district, to be by him transmitted to the Treasury Board, the deputy commissary general shall no longer be chargeable or accountable for the good behavior of such assistants.

3. That every deputy commissary general shall be authorized to appoint as many clerks, not exceeding the number of three, as the respective commissaries general shall judge necessary, who are directed to report the same to Congress.

4. And whereas it is represented that it will be exceeding difficult to comply with the regulations of Congress, for branding and numbering cattle on the horns: *Resolved,* That the purchasers of live stock be respectively directed to adopt such

other modes for marking the same as they shall judge expedient, and to transmit to Congress, by the earliest opportunity, the regulations for that purpose by them adopted:

5. That the Commissary General of purchases be directed to inform the Deputy Commissary General of purchases for the eastern District, that the Regulations of Congress requiring the Receipts of the issuing Commissaries as Vouchers to the Accounts of the purchases of Cattle are necessary, as well to ascertain the Weight of the Meat, Hides, and Tallow wch the sd issuing Commissaries are respectively to account for, as to inform Congress with the Cost thereof, and therefore that the said Regulations can by no Means be disposed with.

5a. That each of the deputy commissaries general of purchases be authorized to allow to the purchasers of live stock, in his respective district, a longer time for making the returns required by the 10th article of the regulations of the departments of the commissaries, than is thereon specified; provided such deputy commissary general shall judge it necessary, and the time further allowed does not exceed one month. And if, in the hurry of a march or engagement, or at any other time, any deputy appointed to receive, kill, and deliver live stock, shall be unable to weigh the meat, hides, and tallow thereof, he shall be indemnified from any charge of neglect, upon producing to the respective purchaser of cattle, a certificate from the commanding officer of the army, post, or detachment, of the fact as aforesaid; and such certificate shall also excuse the purchaser of live stock from producing the receipt of the issuing commissary, required by the 14th article of the said regulations:

6. *Resolved,* That it never was the Intention of Congress, by any of the regulations of the Commissarys Departments, to charge the Loss of Cattle on the Road, or straying from their Keepers at the Camp, to the purchaser of Live Stock, or any officer of the Department unless when the Officers on whom it was incumbent, shall not have taken proper and reasonable Care, according to the Circumstances of the place, post, or Magazine, for the Security of such Cattle.

[This last paragraph subsequently was stricken out, to be replaced by:]

6. That it never was the intention of Congress to make any purchaser of live stock, or officer of the department, liable for unavoidable loss of all or any part of such live stock, when such purchaser or officer shall make appear that proper care hath been taken to prevent such loss.

Sources

THERE IS no need to apologize for the retelling of a good story; but the reader is entitled to know where the information came from, how it can be checked.

All of the sources of this book are available. There is no new material. Diaries and contemporary letters were much used, as were standard histories and the biographies of persons concerned. A large number of historical-society papers were perused; but these must be taken with care, since grandfather's knee, while perhaps comfortable, is not a reliable fount of history, and amateurs with fond memories and fierce family pride—but no training—sometimes let their enthusiasm carry them to curious places. However, some articles are listed below.

The works that were most frequently consulted are works arranged chronologically, and well indexed, so there seems no reason to clutter this book with notes. Any unacknowledged quotation or paraphrase can be found in one of these:

Correspondence of the American Revolution; being Letters of Eminent Men to George Washington, ed. by Jared Sparks, 4 vols. Boston: Little, Brown and Co., 1853.

Journals of the Continental Congress, 1774-1789, ed. by Worthington Chauncey Ford, 36 vols. Washington: U.S. Government Printing Office, 1904.

Letters of Members of the Continental Congress, ed. by Edumnd C. Burnett, 8 vols. Washington: Carnegie Institute of Washington, 1921-1936.

The Diplomatic Correspondence of the American Revolution, ed. by Jared Sparks, 12 vols. Boston: Nathan Hale and Gray & Bowen, 1830.

The Writings of George Washington, from the Original Manuscript Sources, 1745-1799, edited by John Clement Fitzpatrick, 39 vols. Washington: U.S. Government Printing Office, 1931-1944.

Books that are referred to in notes, together with some that were useful, follow:

ABBOTT, JOHN S. C. *George Washington, or, Life in America One Hundred Years Ago.* New York: Dodd Mead & Co., 1875.

ADAMS, CHARLES FRANCIS, ed. *Familiar Letters of John Adams and His Wife Abigail Adams, During the Revolution.* New York: Hurd and Houghton, 1876.

ADAMS, CHARLES FRANCIS. *Studies Military and Diplomatic, 1775-1865.* New York: The Macmillan Co., 1911.

ADAMS, CHARLES FRANCIS, ed. *The Works of John Adams, With Life,* 10 vols. Boston: Little, Brown and Co., 1850-56.

ADAMS, JAMES T. *The Adams Family.* New York: The Literary Guild, 1930.

ALDEN, JOHN RICHARD. *General Charles Lee: Traitor or Patriot?.* Baton Rouge: Louisiana State University Press, 1951.

ALDEN, JOHN RICHARD. *The American Revolution: 1775-1783.* New York: Harper and Brothers, 1954.

ALLEN, GARDNER W. *A Naval History of the American Revolution,* 2 vols. Boston and New York: Houghton Mifflin Co., 1913.

ANDERSON, TROYER STEELE. *The Command of the Howe Brothers During the American Revolution.* New York and London: Oxford University Press, 1936.

ANDRÉ, JOHN. See LODGE, also SARGENT.

ARNOLD, ISAAC N. *Life of Benedict Arnold.* Chicago: Jansen McClurg, 1880.

AUSTIN, JAMES TRECOTHICK, *The Life of Elbridge Gerry, With Contemporary Letters to the Close of the American Revolution,* 2 vols. Boston: Wealls and Lilly, 1828-29.

AZOY, LT. COL. A.C.B. "Monmouth: The Battle That was Won at Valley Forge," *Infantry Journal,* Vol. 46, No. 1.

BAKER, WILLIAM SPOHN. *Itinerary of General Washington from June 15, 1775, to December 23, 1783.* Philadelphia: J. B. Lippincott Company, 1892.

BAKER, WILLIAM SPOHN. *The Camp by the Old Gulph Mill,* address delivered before the Pennsylvania Society of the Sons of the American Revolution. Pennsylvania Magazine of History and Biography, n.d.

BALCH, THOMAS. *The French in America During the War of Independence of the United States, 1777-1783,* 2 vols., a translation by Thomas Willing Balch of *Les Français en Amérique Pendant la Guerre de l'Indépendance des Etats-Unis.* Philadelphia: Porter and Coates, 1891.

BALDWIN, ALICE M. *The New England Clergy and the American Revolution.* Durham, N.C.: Duke University Press, 1928.

BANCROFT, GEORGE. *History of the United States of America,* 6 vols. New York: D. Appleton and Co., 1883.

BARNES, ROBERT HATFIELD. *United States Submarines.* New Haven, Conn.: H. F. Morse Associates, 1944.

BAUERMEISTER. See UHLENDORF.

BEAN, THEODORE W. *Washington At Valley Forge, A Hundred Years Ago.* Norristown, Pa., 1876.

BEDOYERE, MICHAEL DE LA. *George Washington.* Philadelphia: J. B. Lippincott Co., 1935.

BELCHER, HENRY. *The First American Civil War,* 2 vols. London: The Macmillan Co., 1911.

BEMIS, SAMUEL FLAGG. *The Diplomacy of the American Revolution.* New York: D. Appleton-Century Co., 1935.

BILL, ALFRED HOYT. "Drillmaster at Valley Forge," *American Heritage,* June, 1955.

BILL, ALFRED HOYT. *Valley Forge: The Making of an Army.* New York: Harper and Brothers, 1952.

BEVERIDGE, ALBERT J. *The Life of John Marshall,* 2 vols. Boston and New York: Houghton Mifflin Co., 1929.

BEZANSON, ANNE, AND ASSOCIATES. *Prices and Inflation During the American Revolution: Pennsylvania, 1770-90.* Philadelphia: University of Pennsylvania Press, 1951.

BLUMENTHAL, WALTER HART. *Women Camp Followers of the American Revolution.* Philadelphia: George S. MacManus Company, 1952.

BOLTON, CHARLES KNOWLES. *The Private Soldier Under Washington.* New York: Charles Scribner's Sons, 1902.

BOORSTIN, DANIEL J. *The Americans: The Colonial Experience.* New York: Random House, 1958.

BOTTA, CHARLES. *History of the War of Independence of the United States,* 2 vols. New Haven, Conn.: Whiting, 1837.

BOWEN, CATHERINE DRINKER. *John Adams and the American Revolution.* Boston: Little, Brown and Co., 1950.

BOYD, THOMAS. *Mad Anthony Wayne.* New York: Charles Scribner's Sons, 1929.

BROOKS, NOAH. *Henry Knox, a Soldier of the Revolution.* New York: G. P. Putnam's Sons, 1900.

BURNETT, EDMUND C. *The Continental Congress.* New York: The Macmillan Co., 1941.

BUTTERFIELD, L. H. *Letters of Benjamin Rush,* 2 vols. Princeton, N. J.: Princeton University Press, 1951.

CALLAHAN, NORTH. *Henry Knox: General Washington's General.* New York: Rinehart and Co., 1958.

CARRINGTON, HENRY G. *Washington the Soldier,* 2nd ed. New York: Charles Scribner's Sons, 1899.

CHANNING, EDWARD. *A History of the United States,* 6 vols. New York: The Macmillan Co., 1825.

CHINARD, GILBERT, ed. *George Washington as the French Knew Him*. Princeton, N. J.: Princeton University Press, 1940.

CLARK, DORA MAE. *British Opinion and the American Revolution*. New Haven, Conn.: Yale University Press, 1930.

CLARK, GEORGE LARKIN. *Silas Deane, a Connecticut Leader in the American Revolution*. New York and London: G. P. Putnam's Sons, 1913.

CORWIN, EDWARD S. *French Policy and the American Alliance of 1778*. Princeton, N. J.: Princeton University Press, 1916.

CURTIS, EDWARD E. *Organization of the British Army in the American Revolution*. New Haven, Conn.: Yale University Press, 1926.

CUNLIFFE, MARCUS. *George Washington: Man and Monument*. Boston: Little, Brown and Co., 1958.

DALSÊME, RENÉ. *Beaumarchais, 1732-1799,* tr. by Hannaford Bennett. New York: G. P. Putnam's Sons, 1929.

DAVIDSON, PHILIP. *Propaganda and the American Revolution, 1763-1783*. Chapel Hill, N. C.: University of North Carolina Press, 1941.

DEANE, SILAS. *The Deane Papers,* 5 vols. New York: The New-York Historical Society, 1887-1891.

DEARBORN, HENRY. "Journal," *Proceedings of the Massachusetts Historical Society 1886,* 2nd series, vol. 2.

DOYLE, JOSEPH B. *Frederick William Von Steuben and the American Revolution*. Steubenville, Ohio: The H. C. Cook Co., 1913.

DRAKE, FRANCIS SAMUEL. *Life and Correspondence of Henry Knox*. Boston: S. G. Drake, 1873.

EWEN, DAVID. *Music Comes to America*. New York: Towne and Heath, 1947.

FISHER, SYDNEY GEORGE. *The Struggle for American Independence,* 2 vols. Philadelphia: J. B. Lippincott Co., 1908.

FISK, JOHN. *The American Revolution,* 2 vols. Boston and New York: Houghton Mifflin Co., 1891.

FITZPATRICK, JOHN CLEMENT. *George Washington Himself: a Common-Sense Biography Written from his Manuscripts*. Indianapolis: Bobbs, Merrill Co., 1933.

FITZPATRICK, JOHN CLEMENT. *The Spirit of the Revolution: New Light from Some of the Original Sources of American History*. Boston and New York: Houghton Mifflin Co., 1924.

FIELD, CYRIL. *The Story of the Submarine*. Philadelphia: J. B. Lippincott Co., n.d.

FORD, HENRY JONES. *Washington and his Colleagues*. New Haven, Conn.: Yale University Press, 1921.

FORD, PAUL LEICESTER. "Dr. Rush and General Washington," *Atlantic Monthly,* Vol. 75, 1895.

FORD, PAUL LEICESTER. *The True George Washington.* Philadelphia: J. B. Lippincott Co., 1896.

FORD, WORTHINGTON CHAUNCEY. "Defences of Philadelphia in 1777," *Pennsylvania Magazine of History and Biography,* vols. XIX, XX and XXI.

FORD, WORTHINGTON CHAUNCEY. "Washington at the Crisis of the Revolutionary War," *Century Magazine,* vol. 18, 1911.

FORTESCUE, J. W. "A Chapter on Red Coats," *Macmillan's Magazine,* Vol. LXVIII, September, 1893.

FORTESCUE, J. W. *History of the British Army,* 10 vols. New York: The Macmillan Company, 1899-1920.

FREEMAN, DOUGLAS SOUTHALL. *George Washington: a Biography,* 6 vols. New York: Charles Scribner's Sons, 1948-54.

FROTHINGHAM, RICHARD. *The Rise of the Republic of the United States.* Boston: Little, Brown and Co., 1910.

FROTHINGHAM, THOMAS G. *Washington: Commander in Chief.* Boston and New York: Houghton Mifflin Co., 1930.

GANOE, WILLIAM ADDLEMAN. *The History of the United States Army,* revised ed. New York and London: D. Appleton-Century Co., 1943.

GARDINER, ASA BIRD. "General James M. Varnum of the Continental Army," *Magazine of American History,* XVIII, September, 1887.

GARDINER, ASA BIRD. "The Uniforms of the American Army," *Magazine of American History,* Vol. I, No. 8, August, 1877.

GOODMAN, NATHAN GERSON. *Benjamin Rush, Physician and Citizen, 1746-1813.* Philadelphia: University of Pennsylvania Press, 1934.

GOTTSCHALK, LOUIS R. *Lafayette Joins the American Army.* Chicago: University of Chicago Press, 1937.

GOULD, F. J. *Thomas Paine, 1737-1809.* Boston: Small, Maynard and Co., 1925.

GRAHAM, JAMES. *The Life of General Daniel Morgan, of the Virginia Line of the Army of the United States.* New York: Derby and Jackson, 1856.

GREENE, FRANCIS VINTON. *General Greene.* New York: D. Appleton and Co., 1893.

GREENE, FRANCIS VINTON. *The Revolutionary War and the Military Policy of the United States.* New York: Charles Scribner's Sons, 1911.

GREENE, GEORGE WASHINGTON. *The Life of Nathanael Greene, Major-General in the Army of the Revolution,* 3 vols. New York: G. P. Putnam and Son, 1867 (vol. 1); Hurd and Houghton, 1871 (vols. 2 and 3).

HALE, EDWARD EVERETT, and EDWARD E. HALE JR. *Franklin in France.* Boston: Roberts Brothers, 1887.

HAMMOND, OTIS A., ed. *Letters and Papers of Major-General*

John Sullivan, Continental Army, 3 vols. Concord, N. H.: The New Hampshire Historical Society, 1930.

HASTINGS, GEORGE EVERETT. *The Life and Works of Francis Hopkinson*. Chicago: The University of Chicago Press, 1926.

HATCH, LOUIS CLINTON. *The Administration of the American Revolutionary Army*. New York: Longmans, Green, and Co., 1904.

HENDRICK, BURTON J. *The Lees of Virginia: Biography of a Family*. Boston: Little, Brown and Co., 1941.

HERR, JOHN K. and EDWARD S. WALLACE. *The Story of the U.S. Cavalry*. Boston: Little, Brown and Co., 1953.

HOSMER, J. K. *Samuel Adams*. Boston: Houghton Mifflin Co., 1885.

HOW, DAVID. *Diary*. Morrisania, N. Y.: privately printed, 1865.

HOWARD, JOHN TASKER. *Our American Music: Three Hundred Years of It*. New York: Thomas Y. Crowell Co., 1930.

HUGHES, RUPERT. *George Washington,* 3 vols. New York: William Morrow and Co., 1930.

HUTCHINSON, J. R. *The Press Gang, Afloat and Ashore*. New York: E. P. Dutton and Co., 1914.

INGRAHAM, EDWARD D. *Papers in Relation to the Case of Silas Deane*. Philadelphia: T. K. and P. G. Collins, 1855.

IRVING, WASHINGTON. *The Life of Washington,* 3 vols. New York: Frank F. Lovell Co., 1856.

JACOBS, JAMES RIPLEY. *Tarnished Warrior: Major-General James Wilkinson*. New York: The Macmillan Company, 1938.

JOHNSON, WILLIAM. *Sketches of the Life and Correspondence of Nathanael Greene, Major General of the Armies of the United States in the War of the Revolution,* 2 vols. Charleston, S. C.: published by the author, 1822.

JORDAN, JOHN W. "The Military Hospitals at Bethlehem and Lititz during the Revolution," *The Pennsylvania Magazine of History and Biography,* Vol. XX, No. 2.

KAPP, FRIEDRICH. *The Life of Frederick William von Steuben, Major General in the Revolutionary Army,* 2nd ed. New York: Mason Brothers, 1859.

KAPP, FRIEDRICH. *The Life of John Kalb, Major-General in the Revolutionary Army*. New York: Henry Holt and Co., 1884.

KITE, ELIZABETH S. *Beaumarchais and the War of American Independence,* 2 vols. Boston: Richard G. Badger, 1918.

KITE, ELIZABETH S. *Brigadier-General Louis Lebègue Duportail, Commandant of Engineers in the Continental Army, 1777-1783.* Baltimore: The Johns Hopkins Press, 1933.

KNOLLENBERG, BERNHARD. *John Adams, Knox, and Washington.* Worcester, Mass.: American Antiquarian Society, 1947.

KNOLLENBERG, BERNHARD. *Washington and the Revolution: a Reappraisal.* New York: The Macmillan Co., 1940.

KNOX, DUDLEY W. *The Naval Genius of George Washington.* Boston: Houghton Mifflin Co., 1932.

LAURENS, JOHN. See SIMMS.

LECKY, W. E. H. *History of England in the Eighteenth Century*, 8 vols. London: Longmans, Green and Co., 1878-1890.

LEE, CHARLES. *Memoirs of the Life of the Late Charles Lee, Esq.* London: J. S. Jordan, 1792.

LEE, RICHARD H. *Memoirs of the Life of Richard Henry Lee, and His Correspondence*, 2 vols. Philadelphia: H. C. Carey and I. Lea, 1825.

LEFFERTS, CHARLES M. *Uniforms of the American, British, French, and German Armies in the War of the American Revolution, 1775-1783*, ed. by Alexander J. Wall. New York: the New-York Historical Society, 1926.

LITTLE, SHELBY. *George Washington*. New York: Minton, Balch and Co., 1929.

LIVELY, ROBERT A. See WADE, HERBERT T.

LODGE, HENRY CABOT, ed. *André's Journal*, 2 vols. Boston: The Bibliophile Society, 1903.

LOWELL, EDWARD J. *The Hessians and the Other German Auxiliaries of Great Britain in the Revolutionary War*. New York: Harper and Brothers, 1884.

MACLAY, EDGAR STANTON. *A History of American Privateers*. New York and London: D. Appleton and Co., 1926.

MAHAN, A. T. *The Major Operations of the Navies in the War of American Independence*. London: Sampson Low, Marston and Co., 1913.

MANROSS, WILLIAM WILSON. *A History of the American Episcopal Church*. New York and Milwaukee: Morehouse Publishing Co., 1935.

MARTIN, LOUIS. *George Washington*. New York: Thomas Y. Crowell Co., 1932.

MARX, RUDOLPH. "A Medical Profile of George Washington," *American Heritage*, August, 1955.

MASEFIELD, JOHN. *Sea Life in Nelson's Time*. New York: The Macmillan Co., 1937.

MATTHEWS, ALBERT. "Uncle Sam," *Proceedings of the American Antiquarian Society*, new series, Vol. XIX, 1909.

MCMICHAEL, JAMES. "The Diary of Lieutenant James McMichael, of the Pennsylvania Line, 1776-1778," *The Pennsylvania Magazine of History and Biography*, Vol. XVI, No. 2, 1892.

MILLER, JOHN C. *Sam Adams*. Boston: Little, Brown and Co., 1936.

MONTRESOR. See SCULL.

MONTROSS, LYNN. *Rag, Tag and Bobtail: The Story of the Continental Army*. New York: Harper and Brothers, 1952.

MONTROSS, LYNN. *The Reluctant Rebels: The Story of the Continental Congress*. New York: Harper and Brothers, 1950.

MOORE, FRANK. *Songs and Ballads of the American Revolution*. New York: D. Appleton and Co., 1856.

MOORE, GEORGE H. *The Treason of Charles Lee.* New York: Charles Scribner's Sons, 1860.

MORSE, JOHN T., JR. *Benjamin Franklin.* Boston: Houghton Mifflin Co., 1891.

MORSE, JOHN T., JR. *John Adams.* Boston: Houghton Mifflin Co., 1899.

NETTELS, CURTIS P. *George Washington and American Independence.* Boston: Little, Brown and Co., 1951.

NEVINS, ALLAN. *The American States During and after the Revolution, 1775-1789.* New York: The Macmillan Co., 1927.

NICKERSON, HOFFMAN. *The Turning Point of the Revolution, or, Burgoyne in America.* Boston: Houghton Mifflin Co., 1928.

OBERHOLTZER, ELLIS PAXSON. *Robert Morris: Patriot and Financier.* New York: The Macmillan Co., 1903.

O'BRIEN, MICHAEL J. "Washington's Irish Friends," *Journal of the American Irish Historical Society,* Vol. XXV.

PINKOWSKI, EDWARD. *Washington's Officers Slept Here: Historic Homes of Valley Forge and its Neighborhood.* Philadelphia: The Sunshine Press, 1953.

PAINE, THOMAS. See WHEELER.

PALMER, JOHN MCAULEY. *General von Steuben.* New Haven: Yale University Press, 1937.

PARTRIDGE, BELLAMY. *Sir Billy Howe.* London and New York: Longmans, Green and Co., 1932.

PECKHAM, HOWARD H. *The War for Independence: A Military History.* Chicago: University of Chicago Press, 1958.

PERKINS, JAMES BRECK. *France and the American Revolution.* Boston: Houghton Mifflin Co., 1911.

PICKERING, OCTAVIUS. See UPHAM.

PRESTON, JOHN HYDE. *A Gentleman Rebel: The Exploits of Anthony Wayne.* New York: Farrar and Rinehart, 1930.

RANKIN. See SCHEER.

RAWLE, WILLIAM. "Sketch of the Life of Thomas Mifflin," *Historical Society of Pennsylvania, Memoirs,* Vol. II, Part 2, 1827.

RITCHESON, CHARLES R. *British Politics and the American Revolution.* Norman, Okla.: University of Oklahoma Press, 1954.

ROBSON, ERIC. *The American Revolution in its Political and Military Aspects, 1763-1783.* London: The Batchworth Press, 1955.

ROOSEVELT, THEODORE. *Gouverneur Morris.* Boston and New York: Houghton Mifflin Co., 1891.

ROSEMAN, KENNETH R. *Thomas Mifflin and the Politics of the American Revolution.* Chapel Hill, N. C.: The University of North Carolina Press, 1952.

ROSSITER, CLINTON. *Seedtime of the Republic: The Origin of the American Tradition of Political Liberty.* New York: Harcourt, Brace and Co., 1953.

ROWLAND, KATE MASON. *The Life of Charles Carroll of Carrollton,* 2 vols. New York and London: G. P. Putnam's Sons, 1899.

RUSH, BENJAMIN. See GOODMAN, also FORD, P. L.

RUSSELL, PHILLIPS. *Benjamin Franklin: The First Civilized American.* New York: Brentano's, 1927.

SARGENT, WINTHROP. *The Life and Career of Major André, Adjutant-General of the British Army in America.* Boston: Ticknor and Fields, 1861.

SAWYER, CHARLES WINTHROP. *Firearms in American History, 1600-1800.* Boston: published by the author, 1910.

SAWYER, JOSEPH DILLAWAY. *Washington,* 2 vols. New York: The Macmillan Co., 1927.

SCHACHNER, NATHAN. *Alexander Hamilton.* New York: D. Appleton-Century Co., 1946.

SCHLESINGER, ARTHUR MEIER. *The Colonial Merchants and the American Revolution.* New York: Facsimile Library, 1939.

SCHEER, GEORGE F., and HUGH F. RANKIN. *Rebels and Redcoats.* Cleveland and New York: The World Publishing Co., 1957.

SCOTT, KENNETH. *Counterfeiting in Colonial America.* New York: Oxford University Press, 1957.

SCULL, G. D., ed. *The Montresor Journals.* New York: The New-York Historical Society, 1881.

SIMMS, WILLIAM G., ed. *The Army Correspondence of Col. John Laurens in the Years 1777-8 to his Father, etc.* New York: Bradford Club, 1867.

SIMMS, WILLIAM G. *The Life of Nathanael Greene, Major-General in the Army of the Revolution.* Philadelphia: Leary and Getz, 1849.

SONNECK, OSCAR GEORGE THEODORE. *Report on 'The Star-Spangled Banner,' 'Hail Columbia,' 'America,' 'Yankee Doodle.'* Washington: U.S. Government Printing Office, 1909.

STEDMAN, CHARLES. *The History of the Origin, Progress, and Termination of the American War,* 2 vols. London: printed for the author, 1794.

STEUBEN, WILHELM VON. *Regulations for the Order and Discipline of the Troops of the United States.* Boston: Thomas and Andrews, 1794.

STEWART, FRANK H. "Foraging for Valley Forge," *New Jersey Historical Society Proceedings,* new series, Vol. 17.

STILLÉ, CHARLES J. The Comte de Broglie, proposed Stadholder of America," *Pennsylvania Magazine of History and Biography,* Vol. XI.

SULLIVAN, JOHN. See HAMMOND.

SUMNER, CHARLES GRAHAM. *The Financier and the Finances of the American Revolution,* 2 vols. New York: Dodd, Mead and Co., 1891.

SWEET, WILLIAM WARREN. *Religion in Colonial America.* New York: Charles Scribner's Sons, 1942.

SWIGGETT, HOWARD. *The Extraordinary Mr. Morris.* Garden City, N. Y.: Doubleday and Co., 1952.

TAYLOR, FRANK H. *Valley Forge: a Chronicle of American Heroism.* Philadelphia: James N. Nagle, 1905.

THACHER, JAMES. *Military Journal During the American Revolutionary War.* Boston: Richardson and Lord, 1823.

THAYER, WILLIAM ROSCOE. *George Washington.* Boston: Houghton Mifflin Co., 1922.

THORTON, JOHN WINGATE, ed. *The Pulpit of the American Revolution, or, the Political Sermons of the Period of 1776.* Boston: D. Lothrop and Co., 1876.

TOWER, CHARLEMAGNE, JR. *The Marquis de La Fayette in the American Revolution,* 2 vols. Philadelphia: J. B. Lippincott Co., 1895.

TREVELYAN, GEORGE OTTO. *The American Revolution,* 6 vols. London: Longmans, Green and Co., 1905.

TRUMBULL, JOHN. *Autobiography, Reminiscences and Letters, from 1756 to 1841.* New Haven, Conn.: B. L. Hamlen, 1841.

TRUMBULL, JONATHAN. *Jonathan Trumbull, Governor of Connecticut, 1769-1784.* Boston: Little, Brown and Co., 1919.

TYLER, MOSES COIT. *Patrick Henry.* Boston: Houghton Mifflin Co., 1898.

TYLER, MOSES COIT. *The Literary History of the American Revolution,* 2 vols. New York: G. P. Putnam's Sons, 1897.

UHLENDORF, BERNHARD A., and EDNA VOSPER, eds. *Letters from Major Baurmeister to Colonel von Jungkenn, Written during the Philadelphia Campaign, 1777-1778.* Philadelphia: Historical Society of Pennsylvania, 1937.

UHLENDORF, BERNHARD A., ed. *Revolution in America: Confidential Letters and Journals, 1776-1784, of Adjutant General Major Baurmeister of the Hessian Forces.* New Brunswick, N. J.: Rutgers University Press, 1957.

UPHAM, CHARLES WENTWORTH, and OCTAVIUS PICKERING. *The Life of Timothy Pickering,* 4 vols. Boston: Little, Brown and Co., 1867-1873.

VAN DOREN, CARL. *Benjamin Franklin.* New York: The Viking Press, 1938.

VAN DOREN, CARL. *Secret History of the American Revolution.* New York: The Viking Press, 1941.

VAN TYNE, CLAUDE HALSTEAD. "Influence of the Clergy, and of Religious and Sectarian Forces, on the American Revolution," *American Historical Review,* XIX, 1914.

VAN TYNE, CLAUDE HALSTEAD. "Influences Which Determined the French Government to Make the Treaty with America, 1778," *American Historical Review,* April, 1916.

VAN TYNE, CLAUDE HALSTEAD. *The War of Independence: American Phase.* Boston and New York: Houghton Mifflin Co., 1929.

VAN TYNE, CLAUDE HALSTEAD. *The Loyalists in the American Revolution.* New York: Peter Smith, 1929.

VER STEEG, CLARENCE L. *Robert Morris: Revolutionary Financier.* Philadelphia: University of Pennsylvania Press, 1954.

VOSPER, EDNA. See UHLENDORF.

WADE, HERBERT T. and ROBERT A. LIVELY. *This Glorious Cause: The Adventures of Two Company Officers in Washington's Army.* Princeton, N. J.: Princeton University Press, 1958.

WALDO, ALBIGENCE. "Diary Kept at Valley Forge," *Pennsylvania Magazine of History and Biography,* Vol. XXI.

WALL, ALEXANDER. See LEFFERTS.

WALLACE, EDWARD S. See HERR.

WALSH, CORREA MOYLAN. *The Political Science of John Adams.* New York: G. P. Putnam's Sons, 1915.

WALTON, JOSEPH S. "George Washington in Chester County," *Proceedings of the Chester County Historical Society for 1898.*

WARD, CHRISTOPHER. *The War of the Revolution,* 2 vols. New York: The Macmillan Co., 1952.

WHARTON, FRANCIS. *Revolutionary Correspondence of the United States,* 6 vols. Washington: U.S. Government Printing Office, 1889.

WHITELEY, WILLIAM G. *The Revolutionary Soldiers of Delaware.* Wilmington, Del.: James and Webb, 1875.

WHITLOCK, BRAND. *La Fayette,* 2 vols. New York: D. Appleton and Co., 1929.

WILD, EBENEZER. "Journal, 1776-1781," *Proceedings of the Massachusetts Historical Society,* second series, Vol. VI, October, 1890.

WILDES, HARRY EMERSON. *Valley Forge.* New York: The Macmillan Co., 1938.

WILKINSON, JAMES. *Memoirs of My Own Times,* 3 vols. Philadelphia: Abraham Small, 1816.

WOODMAN, HENRY. *The History of Valley Forge,* 3rd ed. Oaks, Pa.: J. U. Francis, Sr., 1922.

WOODWARD, WILLIAM E. *George Washington: The Image and the Man.* New York: Boni and Liveright, 1926.

WOODWARD, WILLIAM E. *Tom Paine: America's Godfather. 1737-1809.* New York: E. P. Dutton and Co., 1945.

WRONG, GEORGE M. *Washington and His Comrades in Arms.* New Haven: Yale University Press, 1921.

Index